Fresh from the Farm

Fresh from the Farm

GREAT LOCAL FOODS FROM NEW YORK STATE

A guide to the best shops and farms, with recipes

Susan Meisel & Nathalie Sann

FOREWORD BY DAVID WALTUCK

RIZZOLI
NEW YORK

New York Paris London Milan

First published in the United States of America in 2010
by Rizzoli International Publications, Inc.
300 Park Avenue South
New York, NY 10010
www.rizzoliusa.com

2010 2011 2012 2013 / 10 9 8 7 6 5 4 3 2 1

Editor: Chris Steighner
Design by Lynne Yeamans/Lync

Printed in China

ISBN: 978-0-7893-2031-5

Library of Congress Control Number: 2009940172

To Louis, Ari, and Anna
—Susan Meisel

To my family
—Nathalie Sann

Contents

Foreword

Susan Meisel and Nathalie Sann, the co-authors of this book, are generous cooks and passionate eaters. They also possess a rare appreciation for both sides of the culinary equation: both raw ingredients and the cuisine into which, in the right hands, those ingredients can be transformed. They are the kind of people for whom chefs love to cook and also the kind of people farmers have in mind as they nurture their crops—because Susan and Nathalie are so fully equipped to enjoy and to share the fruits of their labor.

This book, with its portraits of farmers and artisans, cheese-makers and vintners—not to mention insider's recipes, Susan's evocative photographs, and Nathalie's informative writing—confirms my theory. In the pages that follow, you will be treated to a taste of the enthusiasm and expertise that Susan and Nathalie's friends have cherished for years. Whether it inspires you to road-trip around New York State and experience the depicted destinations for yourself, or simply to savor the virtual visits, I dare say you will be enriched by the passion on display here, and that of the people they profile.

It was Susan's love of food and dining that first brought us together. My wife and business partner, Karen, and I were sitting in the unfinished dining room of Chanterelle restaurant late one evening, exhausted after one of many long days spent converting an old bodega into the restaurant of our dreams. Then Susan—on roller skates!—appeared in our front door, drawn there by her natural sense of curiosity, especially where food and restaurants were concerned.

Long before fashionable restaurants began trumpeting sources of vegetables, meats, and cheeses on their menus, Susan and Nathalie understood that great ingredients make great meals. Nathalie, a superb cook, brought her finely honed food-ferreting skills to New York from Paris, and Susan has spent her life photographing the food stores in New York City and Long Island. I vividly remember a weekend visit to Susan's Long Island home almost twenty years ago, when she prepared a salad made with some of the most extraordinary tomatoes I'd ever tasted—juicy, sweet, fragrant, and the source of a standard-setting memory that abides to this day.

This book is a must-have for those wishing to buy local and eat fresh foods. *Fresh from the Farm* is the ultimate expression of passion for food, quality, and generosity. I urge you to explore it as you would the highways and byways of New York—browsing at your own pace, and stopping at the places that pique your interest. But do yourself a favor and read at least a little about each of the farms and what they have to offer. Susan and Nathalie know their stuff and after you've completed this delicious tour of the Empire State, so will you.

—DAVID WALTUCK
New York City
November 2009

Introduction

The idea for this book grew out of our inadvertent discovery of the locavore movement while researching our first book, *Gourmet Shops of New York*. *Gourmet Shops* focused on small, quality food producers and purveyors throughout the five boroughs of New York City, and one section of the book was devoted to the Union Square Market.

There we met the farmers, fishermen, cheese makers, and bakers who trucked in their wares from places pretty much unknown to us—aka The Land Beyond the Five Boroughs. (We were both familiar with the South Fork of Long Island, but mostly as a sort of Summer Borough of New York City.)

It was from the Union Square food folks that we first learned about the local food movement, about how "good to eat" and "good for the environment" go hand in hand. The local food movement is based on the principle of sustainability, which means, roughly, that our food should be grown not only in a healthful way, but in a way that has the least possible negative effect on the overall environment. While organic is great, sustainable goes one step further. For instance, even if you were to grow tomatoes using the strictest organic and biodynamic growing practices—no pesticides, no chemical fertilizers, no genetic engineering, constant care for the soil—but then you shipped those tomatoes all the way across the country, then the net effect on the environment would be harmful, given the gallons of gas burned in the transportation. Things get even worse when you're talking about moving livestock or more perishable foods that require refrigeration across great distances. Eating local is a way to reduce your carbon footprint.

Simply stated, the tenets of the locavore movement are grow it locally, sell it locally, and eat it locally. The generally accepted definition of *local* is food produced within a one-hundred-mile radius of the market. For New York City, the Union Square farmers' market could be seen as the core of the locavore movement. It's located in a central, heavily populated place where isolated local growers can find buyers for their wares. This is not a new idea; every small village in Europe has a market square. But the concept has now found new currency among aware consumers in this country.

We were not converts; we were already believers. For me, having grown up in France, the phrase "local food" was perplexing. Is there any other kind of food? Each region of France is famous for the different kinds of foods produced. Take for example the famous Poulet de Bresse, or Epoisse, which was known as a place before it became synonymous as a kind of cheese. The list goes on and on. France is small enough that all these regional producers can get their food to the bigger cities without much strain on the environment. As for Susan, she'd long been conscious of the benefits of locally grown and produced food.

So our initial view of the movement was, at first, more pragmatic than ideological. We figured anything that could help improve the quality of food generally available in the United States would be beneficial. But as we talked more and more to the people at Union Square Market and tried and retried their products, our quiet acceptance turned into full-on boosterism. We believe the locavore movement will ultimately improve the quality of life and the health of millions of Americans.

We decided to follow those wonderful people we met at the Union Square Market back to their farms, dairies, orchards, and bakeries, then report back on what we found. And we used one of the main tenets of the local food movement as the organizing principle of this book: everything we would photograph and write about would be within a one-hundred-mile radius of the epicenter, Union Square Market.

So, Susan and I jammed into her pickup truck and traveled the country roads of New York State. We had our usual share of false starts, dead ends, and ornery proprietors. At one stop deep in the Catskill forest, we came upon an isolated camp full of men who told us they had not laid eyes on any women for months. We weren't sure whether they were putting us on or not, but we were only too happy to get out of there as quickly as we could. However, for the most part we were met with great warmth and enthusiasm.

Aldo's Café in Greenport, Long Island, was one of those places. The proprietor could hold his own with the great café keepers of Paris. Part chef, part raconteur, part shrink, he told stories, cracked jokes, and commiserated with customers. We felt so at home, so welcome at Aldo's that I started thinking it might be cool to live year-round in Greenport.

We were inspired by the extraordinary success of Community Supported Agriculture groups (CSAs). The CSA movement is about putting the principles of eating local into practice, and getting people into closer touch with the production of their food. Here's how it works: You purchase a share in a particular farm at the beginning of the growing season. Then, every week, the farmer brings a delivery of produce to a designated drop-off point, where all the CSA members come to collect their shares. Some CSA memberships require a stint helping out on the farm, but most simply offer an arranged visit to the farm at one point during the year.

We were struck by the extraordinary beauty and plenty of rural New York State. It was amazing to witness the incredible dedication, passion, and skill of the people who account for the state's local food production. We hope this new book imparts at least a sense of all these wonderful people and places. It is our goal that this book will serve as a guide and inspiration for you to plan a visit and to enjoy the local bounty.

Long Island

In the seventeenth century, Long Island was settled almost simultaneously by the Dutch in Brooklyn at the western end and by the English at Southold on the eastern end. The East End provided a well-stocked larder for the first English settlers who arrived there from Connecticut. The sea was rich with fish and crustaceans, and the treeless expanses of fertile glacial moraine made for superior grazing and farming. Fish literally jumped out of the sea and newly planted crops all but exploded out of the sandy soil. Acres and acres of wild cranberries covered the low dunes, and other berries grew in huge swaths by the sides of narrow paths. Over the years agriculture and fishing grew side by side, forming the mainstays of the East End economy.

For farmers, the fertile soil and temperate weather moderated by the sea made Long Island a perfect place to grow potatoes, wheat, fruits, and vegetables. The fishermen found shoals of oysters, mussels, and clams of all sizes. The waters swarmed with striped bass, bluefish, bonito, flounder, fluke, pollock, and shark. In September schools of alewives in Long Island Sound stretched solid to the horizon.

This rural synergy remained relatively untouched— even as developers gobbled up the farms of western Long Island to house commuters from New York City—until well after World War II.

But in the late 1950s a surge in the area's popularity as a resort combined with falling farm prices put pressure on farmers to sell their land to developers. In 1950 there were three thousand working farms on Long Island; by 2004 only three hundred remained.

The fishing industry also went into steep decline, ruined by years of unchecked overfishing. The vast schools of fish and shoals of shellfish dwindled. Striped bass, once so plentiful they were used to fertilize gardens, became an endangered species (along with once plentiful ospreys, decimated by the effects of DDT). By the beginning of the twenty-first century, farming and fishing on the East End weren't quite dead, but they certainly weren't exactly flourishing.

Recently, a remarkable new energy, emanating from the local foods movement and the North Fork wineries, has brought life back to the farm fields. Over the past twenty-five years the number of vineyards on the East End has gone from zero to thirty, with more than three thousand acres under cultivation. And the amount of acreage used for the production of food has begun to hold steady after years of decline. The fisheries, as a result of sound conservation policy and mindful practice, are also making a comeback.

Blue Point Brewing Company

Like a lot of young men, Mark Buford and Peter Cotter share a passion for beer, but they took their passion way past the simple joy of downing a few cold ones, and became first-rate brewmasters. Mark was an early convert to the homebrew movement; he made beer in his basement using techniques he'd learned online from other home brewers. Peter traveled to Europe, where instead of visiting museums, he stopped off at local breweries, where, little by little, he learned how to make beer the European way.

So when the time came for the two friends to open a business, not surprisingly they launched Blue Point Brewing Company in Patchogue, Long Island, and started brewing some of the best beer you can find anywhere in the world. Their first effort—a lightly toasted lager—won a gold medal at the World Cup for Beer in 2006. Today, Blue Point produces a range of light and dark beers as well as a wonderfully hoppy ale. They sell unpasteurized brew in returnable refill jugs, and you've never tasted ale this fresh and delightful. All their brews are made with barley and hops from Belgium, Canada, and Germany, all organic and not genetically modified.

Peter and Mark will also provide a few tips about which beer to drink with which food: light beer for seafood; dark beer for roasts and red meat; and, for spicy food, a crisp hoppy ale works best.

A stop at the Blue Point tasting room is definitely worth a detour, but make sure you've chosen a designated driver before going in.

Blue Point Brewing Company 161 River Avenue | Patchogue, NY 11772
(631) 475-6944 | www.bluepointbrewing.com

SAUSAGE MADE DAILY

DEL FIORE
PORK & RAVIOLI
COLD CUTS · PASTA · MOZZARELLA

ITALIAN
DELI

Italian
Pork Store

Del Fiore Italian Pork Store

Scotto's Italian Pork Store

Del Fiore Italian Pork Store

This tiny pork store in Hampton Bays is a celebration of great Italian American food. The superb quality of the food offered here and the sheer joy of the place are what separate Scotto's from the hundreds of run-of-the-mill salumerias on Long Island. The front window is full of bright neon, haloing a huge pink plaster pig in a toque surrounded by sausages and canned goods. Inside, the store is packed solid with food—there's barely an empty square inch to put one's feet—with baskets, cheeses, and salamis hanging from the ceiling and display cases and freezers full of homemade pasta, sauces, and prepared foods. Everything here is first rate, and many of the North Fork wineries use Scotto's as their catering supplier.

The pizza is a standout, baked in the wood-burning oven at the back of the store. It's simply made with Scotto's own mozzarella (another must-have), fresh tomatoes, and of course a homemade crust. The result is superb.

Scotto's makes fresh sausage every day. You can find sweet sausages flavored with fennel and hot pepper sausages that will clear your sinuses; you'll find cheese and parsley, lamb, and breakfast sausages, all flavorful and fresh. The fresh ricotta and mascarpone packed away in the refrigerator are as good as we've had anywhere.

In the 1960s and 70s a great many second- and third-generation Italian American families decided to leave behind their grandparents' inner-city Little Italy for a better life in the suburbs. The good news is they took their recipes with them so that little towns like Patchogue, way out on Long Island, are now remarkable sources for first-rate Italian food: dry sausage, pasta fresh and dried, meats, and homemade tomato sauces. Little Italy's loss was Patchogue's gain. And it's in Patchogue you'll find what may well be some of the best mozzarella you will ever taste.

At Del Fiore's, they make four or five fresh batches of mozzarella every weekday, plus ten on weekends. There are no labels on their cheeses; Lorenzo Del Fiore insists that his customers not refrigerate his mozzarella but instead recommends they keep it in a sealed jar. Refrigeration doesn't seem to be a major concern, mostly because a Del Fiore mozzarella never lasts more than ten minutes after it's opened. Serve a slice on grilled bread with just a drop of olive oil, and the rich, milky taste seeps into the bread. The only other way to get mozzarella this good and this fresh would be to live on a buffalo farm outside Naples.

Scotto's Italian Pork Store
25 West Montauk Highway | Hampton Bays, NY 11946
(631) 728-5677 | www.scottosporkstore.com

Del Fiore Italian Pork Store
51 North Ocean Avenue | Patchogue, NY 11772 | (631) 475-6080

Sant Ambroeus

Long a must on chic and bustling upper Madison Avenue, Sant Ambroeus just opened another branch in Greenwich Village. But our favorite is still the store on Southampton Village's quiet Main Street.

Run with cool discipline and a warm heart by Francesca and Hans Pauli, Sant Ambroeus doesn't just feel like Milan, it is Milan: the glass cases filled with artfully arranged, incredibly delicious cakes and cookies; the tubs of gelato, made on the premises from a recipe handed down by the gelato masters of Brunico; the dark wood paneling trimmed with alabaster.

Then there is the coffee bar, perfectly Italian. The marble bar is elbow height so you can stand and enjoy some of the best cappuccino anywhere in the world. The espresso machine sparkles, below austere signs written in untranslated Italian. The waiters wear white shirts, black pants, vest and bow tie—very formal, especially in Southampton. The full restaurant in back of the store, though quite pricey, is always a treat. Among our favorites are the marrons glacés that Francesca makes herself every Christmas. (Hint: It's best to put in your request sometime around Labor Day.) A final word of advice: Don't ask for coffee to go. The only paper here is the beautifully designed pink wrapping and the shopping bags.

Sant Ambroeus 30 Main Street | Southampton, NY 11968
(631) 283-1233 | www.santambroeus.com

The Fudge Company

When we asked the proprietor of this charmingly disheveled little store on Main Street in Southampton why his shop isn't chicly designed like all the others on the block, he replied, "This store's for kids. All they want is candy. You think they want a fancy place?" And he's right—the Fudge Company is for kids. The fudge is fudge-y, the ambience is old-time candy store, and the proprietor— who would only identify himself as Mr. Fudge—is a true candy-store curmudgeon.

Mr. Fudge started his business in 1973, so there's a good chance he knows what kids like. Though what's not to like? He makes fudge with the best butter and chocolate and not much else. It's simple and pure, and the flavor goes on and on. Each year he creates a new "flavor of the summer." Some of those have become classics, like maple walnut marshmallow, and chocolate cheesecake. All are surprisingly subtle and delightfully sweet.

The Fudge Company
67 Main Street | Southampton, NY 11968 | (631) 283-8108

The Blue Duck Bakery Café

The Blue Duck Bakery Café is a great American food success story. Keith Kouris drove a delivery truck for a bakery, and got it into his head that he could make better bread than the stuff he was hauling around. So with the money he earned driving, he bought a tiny deli in Huntington, and night after night Keith practiced his craft in the store's small baking oven. He took classes and apprenticed with other bakers to hone his craft, and opened Blue Duck, about ten years ago. Today Blue Duck is probably the foremost artisanal bread bakery in New York State.

Keith and his wife, Nancy, have truly mastered their craft. They make superb bread, and they have managed to maintain this quality in spite of the rapid growth of their business, no easy feat. You can find the Blue Duck logo in just about any quality food store in New York, in great restaurants, and at the Union Square Farmers' Market. They craft their artisanal breads the traditional way, using unbleached flour, water, sea salt, and natural leavenings, then bake them in very hot ovens imported from Italy. Among their specialties are sour rye, French baguette, pain rustique, Pugliese, and French batard.

FRENCH BAGUETTE

The Blue Duck Bakery Café

30 Hampton Road | Southampton, NY 11968 | (631) 204-1701
56275 Main Road | Southold, NY 11971 | (631) 629-4123 | www.blueduckbakerycafe.com

Tate's Bake Shop

Kathleen King was a cookie prodigy. She started baking cookies at age eleven and today runs a cookie empire from her bake shop on North Sea Road in Southampton. The retail store, which she designed inch by inch, radiates the quiet beauty of a Normandy patisserie, giving not a hint that a few miles away Tate's factory bakery is turning out cookies by the ton, shipping them just about everywhere in the world in their distinctive pastel-filigree boxes.

The good news is that even though Tate's produces cookies on a grand scale, they have not lost their artisanal quality. Kathleen makes sure that only the purest ingredients go into her cookies and that her bakers adhere to her strict standards. So, whether you buy a Tate's chocolate chip cookie at the Southampton shop or at your local supermarket, you can be certain the quality is the same. We tried both to make sure.

Tate's signature cookies are the chocolate chip and oatmeal raisin, with sugar and bittersweet chocolate also among customer favorites. Along with these, you'll find coffee cake, cherry cobbler, rhubarb pie, peach crumb pie, pound cake, large muffins, wheat- and gluten-free brownies, macaroons, and bread pudding, all available at Tate's Bake Shop. The espresso bar is a must. Cookies and coffee in Tate's beautiful garden make for a truly special break in a routine afternoon.

Tate's Bake Shop 43 North Sea Road | Southampton, NY 11968 | (631) 283-9830 | www.tatesbakeshop.com

CHOCOLATE CHIP COOKIES

Yields 4¹/₂ dozen 3-inch cookies

Chocolate chip cookies are Tate's signature item. They are thin and crisp and remain everyone's favorite. Tate's Bake Shop bakes and sells thousands a week and ships them all over the country.

2 cups all-purpose flour

1 teaspoon baking soda

1 teaspoon salt

1 cup salted butter, softened

³/₄ cup sugar

³/₄ cup firmly packed dark brown sugar

1 teaspoon water

1 teaspoon vanilla extract

2 large eggs

2 cups semisweet chocolate chips

1. Preheat the oven to 350 degrees F. Grease two cookie sheets or line with silicone nonstick baking mats.

2. In a large bowl, whisk together the flour, baking soda, and salt.

3. In another large bowl, cream the butter and sugars together. Add the water and vanilla and mix until just combined. Add the eggs and mix lightly. Stir in the flour mixture. Fold in the chocolate chips. Be sure not to overmix the dough.

4. Using two tablespoons or an ice cream scoop, drop the cookies 2 inches apart onto the prepared cookie sheets. Bake for 12 minutes, or until the edges and centers are browned. Remove the cookies to a wire rack to cool.

Hampton Prime Meats

Hampton Prime Meats bills itself as the "Old World Butcher Shop" of the Hamptons, and with the closing of Dreesen's in East Hampton, and the fact that Cromer's is technically a supermarket, this little bit of puffery may actually be true.

Ad claims aside, the meat here is superb. It's all organic and grass-fed, with no added antibiotics or hormones. The dry-aged steaks and handmade sausage are as good as you'll find anywhere, as is the beef for grilling. The prices reflect the care and attention to quality, but everything here is worth the extra expense. Look for a giant fiberglass cow resting out front in the garden, and stop in for some of the best cuts of meat you'll find anywhere.

Hampton Prime Meats 235 North Sea Road | Southampton, NY 11968
(631) 287-4909 | www.hamptonprimemeats.com

LOBSTER
4
38.⁰⁰

FRIED
CRAB
SAND.

LUNCH

Daily Specials

DAILY SPECIALS

PEPPERCORN TUNA ON
    CEASAR 9⁹⁵
SOFT SHELL CRAB PO-BOY ... 9⁹⁵
CHICKEN & VEG FETTUCCINI 7⁹⁵
TERIYAKI SWORD, RICE & VEGGIE .. 8⁹⁵
BLACK'N SWORD PO-BOY 8⁹⁵
    HOT .... SOUPS
NEW ENGLAND 5⁰⁰
VEGETARIAN LENTIL 3⁰⁰
BAYMENS CHOWDER 2⁰⁰

Clamman Seafood Market

The late Paul Kloster was the original Clamman. He drove his truck to the small fishing docks along the shores of Peconic Bay and bought scallops, striped bass, and, of course, clams from the local bay men, and he bought game fish from the deep-sea fishermen who docked at Montauk and Shinnecock Inlet.

When Paul passed away, his wife and children decided to carry on the business, and they've built it from a one-truck operation into one of the finest wholesale and retail markets on the East End. Aside from local fish, they import salmon, Gulf grouper, and pompano directly from fisheries around the world. The shrimp are wild, not farmed—a true rarity these days—and you can really taste the difference. The oyster selection is massive and runs from locally farmed Blue Points, to Japanese imports flown in fresh daily. The service at the market is friendly and efficient, and the family works hard to make sure you get exactly what you need.

The Klosters also operate one of the last commercial clamming boats on Peconic Bay. It leaves every morning at 4 a.m. and returns filled to the gunwales with net sacks of cherrystones and littlenecks.

Clamman Seafood Market 235A North Sea Road | Southampton, NY 11968 | (631) 283-6669 | www.clamman.com

Seven Ponds Orchard

This farm, run by the Kraszewski family, is the pick-it-yourself capital of the Hamptons. In the spring and summer you can help yourself to delicious strawberries, raspberries, and blackberries, and in the fall the apples are ready for picking. The Kraszewskis grow fifteen varieties of apples, and will take the time to teach you the ins and outs of proper picking. It's all in the wrist.

Karen Kraszewski uses the fruits in her sublime jams—apple butter, raspberry, blueberry—and her handmade tarts are excellent.

Seven Ponds also offers a huge selection of seasonal produce: plums, pears, tomatoes, string beans, onions, summer squash, peppers, eggplant, cherries, sweet corn, lettuce, melons, potatoes, and winter squash, all grown right on the farm. In the fall—after picking a few dozen apples and getting lost in the corn maze—Seven Ponds Orchard is the perfect place for a picnic.

Seven Ponds Orchard
65 Seven Ponds Road | Water Mill, NY 11976 | (631) 726-8015

Green Thumb Organic Farm

It's easy to spot the Green Thumb on Route 27, just outside Water Mill. You can't miss the huge thumbs-up sign and yellow and green psychedelic pickup truck painted by William Faulkenberg (aka "the green tagger").

Green Thumb was the first wholly organic farm stand on the East End. In 1978, long before it was fashionable, Bill Halsey decided that good health was more important than good yield, so he switched from conventional to organic farming. The practice is much more demanding, much more time-consuming, with no insecticides, no chemical fertilizers, and no genetically modified seeds. The Halseys make their own compost, and all weeding is done by hand. The results are some of the best vegetables you'll find anywhere.

The Halsey family farmed the same land since 1640, and for a long time they cultivated only potatoes. In the 1960s they switched to vegetables, herbs, fruits, and flowers, and now grow more than three hundred different species. The large variety is fantastic, and everything is raised in small batches, so when you see something you like, grab it. It won't be available again until the next year.

During the summer season, Green Thumb offers pony rides for kids, and every once in a while their prize Scottish Highland cattle show up for a guest appearance.

Green Thumb Organic Farm 829 Montauk Highway | Water Mill, NY 11976 | (631) 726-1900 | www.greenthumborganicfarm.com

Hampton Coffee Company

Hampton Coffee Company roasts its coffee one batch at a time using beans the owners, Jason Belken and Theresa Ireland, import from all over the world. You'll find coffee from Hawaii, Brazil, Jamaica, Guatemala, Costa Rica, Kenya, Tanzania, Ethiopia, and Sumatra. Jason and Theresa buy directly from farmers in these regions so they can be sure they get the pick of the crop. The shop's roast master roasts batches on demand and will even help you design your own special blend.

Stop by early in the morning for a delicious cup of coffee, breathe in the powerful aroma of the roasting beans, gobble down a couple of Hampton Coffee's world-class muffins, and take home a bag of beans. It's a full-on, full-quality coffee experience like no other.

Hampton Coffee Company 869 Montauk Highway | Water Mill, NY 11976
(631) 726-2633 | www.hamptoncoffeecompany.com

Milk Pail

The Halsey family started farming in Bridgehampton somewhere around 1640, and they're still at it. The most recent generation, John and Evelyn Halsey and their daughters Amy and Jennifer, run the Milk Pail. They grow mostly apples—they switched from dairy farming thirty years ago, but didn't bother to change the name of their stand.

The apple farm is uniquely beautiful, with acres and acres of espaliered apple trees running down to sparkling Mecox Bay. The Halseys grow twenty-plus varieties of apples, which they then sell at the farm stand. But the real thrill is picking the apples at the farm.

It's just a short drive from Montauk Highway. Follow the signs, then walk up to the little cabin, where you can sample the varieties open for picking that day, choose the size bag you prefer, pay the appropriate fee, and then go fill it up on your own. It's great fun, and there's nothing like the taste of a perfectly ripe apple plucked right off the tree.

To be sure, this is an apple lover's paradise. U-pick season starts in late August with the semitart Sanso variety and ends in early November with the Pink Ladies. In between you can pick Jonamac, Gala, Cortland, Honeycrisp, Jonagold, Mutsu, Red and Golden Delicious, Winesap, Idared, Fuji, Braeburn, Cameo, and Granny Smith. Even more varieties are on sale at the farm stand, along with Milk Pail's excellent donuts.

In October the pick-your-own privileges extend to the pumpkin fields, where you can find any size imaginable, from a half-pound mini to a 150-pound giant. This is a wonderful farm, one not to be missed.

Milk Pail
Summer operation: 757 Mecox Road | Water Mill, NY 11976
Winter operation: 1346 Montauk Highway | Water Mill, NY 11976 | (631) 537-2565
www.milk-pail.com

PUMPKIN AND CHEESE CROSTINI

Serves 4

Pumpkin's savory side is often neglected. Here the cheese and maple syrup bring out its earthy and nutty flavors. If you have leftover roasted pumpkin, there are many possible uses: tossed with quinoa for a salad, mashed with a little milk for a side dish, or thrown into a curry with lentils. Avoid jack-o'-lantern pumpkins, which have little flavor. Instead go for smaller sugar pumpkins or experiment with the many heirloom varieties that have funky shapes and colors.

---

1 small pumpkin (about 2 pounds)

¼ cup extra-virgin olive oil

Salt

½ loaf peasant bread

4 ounces goat cheese

¼ cup maple syrup (grade B if possible)

---

1. Preheat the oven to 350 degrees F. Split the pumpkin in half with a large heavy knife. Remove the seeds and membrane. Cut into more manageable slices, about 2 inches wide. Slice off the peel with a vegetable peeler or knife, then cut into chunks about 1 inch square.

2. Toss the pumpkin chunks with the olive oil and salt to taste. Roast on a baking sheet for about 30 minutes, turning occasionally with a spatula. The pumpkin should be lightly browned, easily pierced with the tip of a knife, but not yet mushy. Remove from the oven and keep warm.

3. Cut the bread into 1/2-inch-thick slices. Toast in the oven until crunchy but not dry. Spread each slice with some of the goat cheese.

4. On a platter, arrange the bread slices. Top each with some pumpkin chunks, and drizzle with the maple syrup. Serve warm.

Fairview Farm & Mecox Bay Dairy

You'll find the Fairview Farm and Mecox Bay Dairy stand alongside Mecox Road, in Bridgehampton, adjacent to their farmland and pastures, two hundred spectacularly beautiful acres that run from the roadside to the edge of Mecox Bay. By rough estimate the land is worth millions, but owners Harry and Art Halsey aren't selling. The acreage has been in their family for more than three hundred years, and the brothers would rather use it to make cheese, graze cows, and grow vegetables and flowers than turn a quick profit.

The sight of grazing milk cows surrounded by the untouched beauty of the East End stands in stark contrast to the advancing phalanx of McMansions on the other side of the road, a truly chilling reminder of how fragile our agricultural heritage is. The Halseys milk their grass-fed cows in a large open barn and make the cheese in a series of connected barns.

They make only a few varieties, but they make them well. The Atlantic Mist, a soft and creamy cheese much like Camembert, tastes like it was made in Normandy. The Halseys also make two excellent semisoft cheeses, Mecox Sunrise and Shawondasee. The hard cheese Sigit, with a strong cheddar flavor, is delicious paired with an old Bordeaux. Fairview Farms is a locavore's delight, and locals and visitors should all be thankful to the Halseys for their devotion to the land.

Fairview Farm & Mecox Bay Dairy
69 Horsemill Lane | Bridgehampton, NY 11932 | (631) 537-6154 | www.mecoxbaydairy.com

CARAMEL CORN

Yield: About 9 quarts

Some foods are just treats, plain and simple. Fresh and local kernels always pop and taste the best. Fairview sells popping corn all year around. This recipe comes from the famous nutritionist, Dr. Wendy Bazilian.

1¼ cups popping corn

1½ sticks salted butter

1 cup brown sugar

⅓ cup light corn syrup

1 teaspoon salt

1 teaspoon baking soda

1. Preheat the oven to 200 degrees F.

2. Pop the popcorn either in an air popper or the conventional way, on the stovetop. The 1¼ cups of kernels should yield about 8 or 9 quarts of popped corn. Transfer the popcorn to a large roasting pan.

3. In a small saucepan, melt the butter and brown sugar. Add the corn syrup and salt. Bring to a boil and keep at a rolling boil for 5 minutes. Immediately remove from the heat and stir in the baking soda. Pour over the popcorn by drizzling back and forth and stirring with a wooden spoon until evenly distributed.

4. Bake for 1 hour, stirring the caramel corn every 15 minutes. Remove from the oven, let cool for 1 hour, and then stir again.

Hayground Market

This enormous enterprise extends an entire block along Montauk Highway. Its specialty is a lack of specificity: If it grows, you can find it here. Stop by to try the roasted corn. You will be back for more!

Hayground Market

1616 Montauk Highway | Bridgehampton, NY 11932
(631) 537-1676

CAULIFLOWER GRATIN

Serves 8

Gigi Grimstad is an accomplished cook and cookbook author in Nashville. As soon as she gets to her vacation house in Southampton, she starts searching for new ingredients and recipes to feed her large family. Of course, she knows about Long Island cauliflower; it's one of the best-known vegetables grown in the region.

2 cauliflower heads, cut into florets

2 tablespoons butter

3 garlic cloves, minced

¼ cup water

2 eggs

1 (15-ounce) container ricotta cheese

¼ cup milk

Dash of cayenne pepper, or to taste

Freshly ground black pepper

Pinch of ground nutmeg

1 tablespoon chopped fresh Italian parsley

1 cup shredded Parmigiano-Reggiano

1 cup shredded mozzarella

1 cup fresh breadcrumbs

1. Preheat the oven to 400 degrees F. Butter a large quiche pan.

2. Cook the cauliflower in a pan with the butter, garlic, and water over medium heat until lightly browned. In a bowl, combine the eggs, ricotta cheese, milk, cayenne pepper, black pepper to taste, nutmeg, parsley, and Parmigiano-Reggiano.

3. Add the cauliflower to the egg mixture and pour everything into the quiche pan. Combine the mozzarella and breadcrumbs and sprinkle over the top.

4. Bake 15 to 20 minutes, or until the top is golden.

Pierre's

Pierre Weber, the proprietor of Pierre's in Bridgehampton, comes from a long line of Alsatian pastry chefs. He started his career in the family's Alsace bakery, so it's no surprise that the desserts at his Bridgehampton bistro are extraordinary. So extraordinary, in fact, that he decided to open a patisserie right next door.

Weber family legend has it that an eighteenth-century ancestor baked pastries for the French Emperor's army. That might help explain why Pierre's most outstanding offering is the Napoleon (known in France as a mille-feuille). Pierre's version features a light and flaky crust filled with richly flavored cream in one of three flavors—buttercream, vanilla, or strawberry. And even though each pastry is quite large,

it is impossible to share. (For the record, the name *Napoleon* does not really refer to the French emperor, but rather is an English distortion of the pastry's place of origin: Naples.)

One of Pierre's goals is to create a small enclave of French culture in the village of Bridgehampton. A day chez Pierre might go like this: for breakfast, coffee with his excellent flaky croissants, either plain, almond, or chocolate. Next, soup for lunch, with a real French sandwich on a crusty baguette. In late afternoon, take the kids for homemade ice cream and sorbet, and while you're there pick up dessert; the Opera, Allegro, and Chocolate Bombe are sure winners. You can even stop in for a late-evening snack; the store is open until 10 p.m.

Pierre's 2468 Main Street | Bridgehampton, NY 11932 | (631) 537-5110 | www.pierresbridgehampton.com

The Tomato Lady

The Tomato Lady is in business one month a year: August. That's when she puts up her sign, unfolds her aluminum chair and table, and sets out her marvelous tomatoes. She'll tell you that anyone selling tomatoes on the East End in July is getting them from New Jersey, or worse.

The sandy, glacial soil in Sagaponack, where she grows her beautiful beefsteaks, is perfect for tomatoes, but because of the cool ocean air, the growing season is about two weeks behind more inland locations. So just be patient. The Tomato Lady's tomatoes are definitely worth the wait.

The Tomato Lady 291 Main Street | Sag Harbor, NY 11963

Open Minded Organics

Open Minded Organics is truly a local enterprise. The proprietor, David Falkowski, grows and sells his flavorful mushrooms within a five-mile radius of his Sag Harbor home. But in spite of Falkowski's old-fashioned homespun marketing approach, his growing operation is pure science. The "farm" is a Quonset hut–shaped cloning lab where Falkowski and his lab assistants start mushroom spores in sterile Petri dishes. They then put the growing spawn (the fungal equivalent of seed) into straw- and nutrient-filled sacks that they hang from the shed's rafters. Within about a month, the mushrooms begin to grow, and the results are delicious. Falkowski explains that the key to success is his ability to keep the spawn vibrant and clean.

After starting from scratch in 2003, Falkowski now produces roughly three hundred pounds of mushrooms per week, all of which he sells to local restaurants and farm stands. The varieties change with the seasons—king oyster, shiitake, blewitt, chanterelle, and morel are just a few. Although Open Minded Organics is not open to the public, their gourmet and exotic treasures are available at farm stands throughout Long Island. Just be sure to stake your claim early—the mushrooms disappear as soon as they come off the truck.

Opend Minded Organics 720 Butter Lane | Bridgehampton, NY 11932 | (631) 574-8889 | www.openmindedorganics.com

Cromer's Market

Tucked away behind a miniscule parking area on busy Noyac Road, Cromer's is one of the best-kept food secrets of the Hamptons. The butcher shop in this otherwise nondescript, old-school supermarket is world class, and the prices make Cromer's an irresistible bargain. The butchers, all excellent, will cut and trim your choice to perfection. Cromer's New York Strip is a must. The beautifully trimmed butterflied leg of lamb is perfect for barbecue, and the stewing veal for Blanquette de Veau is soft and flavorful.

LIQUID PORK

Lolis Eric Elie, the American barbecue expert, gave us this recipe. Lolis had sent the recipe to a friend who renamed it Liquid Pork, since the meat is meant to be braised until it virtually falls apart. This is not a roast to be sliced. You should buy a pork shoulder, not a ham (which tends to be leaner), and ask for it with the skin on. Boston butt will also work.

Pork shoulder	**Bell peppers, quartered**
Garlic cloves, peeled	**Celery, roughly sliced**
Salt and pepper	**Carrots, cut into chunks**
Cayenne pepper and dried peppers	**Canola oil**
Onions, roughly chopped	**Flour**

1. Preheat the oven to 250 degrees F.

2. Stuff the pork shoulder all over with as much garlic as you can. Season generously with salt, pepper, and cayenne pepper. Use fresh and dried Scotch bonnet peppers, if you can.

3. Place the onions, bell peppers, celery, and carrots in the bottom of a roasting pan.

4. In a large skillet, heat 2 tablespoons oil. Brown the roast on all sides over high heat.

5. Place the roast on top of the vegetables. Place it in the oven and prepare a roux: In the same skillet in which you browned the meat, mix more canola oil and a little flour, to make about 1/2 cup roux. Put that in the bottom of the roasting pan.

6. Return the roast to the oven and forget about it. After several hours, taste it to check the seasonings.

7. The roast is done when it starts to fall apart. Peel off the skin. Place it skin-side-down so that the browned side is up and visible. Turn the heat to the highest temperature and crisp the skin in the oven for a few minutes.

Cromer's Market
3500 Noyac Road | Sag Harbor, NY 11963 | (631) 725-9004

A SMALL FARM WITH
A LITTLE BIT OF EVERYTHING

Cavaniola's Gourmet Cheese Shop

It's not easy to turn heads with a new food store in the Hamptons. Start-ups come and go, and last year's latest and greatest often disappear over the slow winter months. Cavaniola's Gourmet Cheese Shop in Sag Harbor has definitely bucked the trend. It opened about five years ago in a tiny shop next to a hardware store on Route 114, and has quickly become a Hamptons' institution.

Michael Cavaniola started out as an architect, and he brings to the cheese business the tools of his former trade: a precise eye for detail and impeccable taste. Everything in the store has one purpose: to make the cheese-buying experience as user friendly as possible. From the service counters built a few inches lower than usual—better for tasting cheese and conversation—to the beautifully displayed packaged foods, each item is set out with care and intelligence.

Which gets us to the cheese—almost two hundred varieties, and Cavaniola and his wife, Tracey, can talk knowledgeably about every one of them. He takes time with all his customers, letting them taste half a dozen different cheeses before they decide. No hurry here, which means the lines can get a little long. Use the waiting time to strike up a conversation, or just explore the offerings. Cavaniola's is a wonder; they've transformed buying cheese into a memorable experience.

Cavaniola's Gourmet Cheese Shop 89B Division Street | Sag Harbor, NY 11963 | (631) 725-0095

FONDUE "EWE"

Serves 4

In the Alps, fondue is a family dish for a cold winter day. In other places, it is just a fun way to eat bread and cheese. This recipe comes from Michael and Tracey Cavaniola's Gourmet Cheese Shop in Sag Harbor. Accompany with crusty bread, cured ham, and dried figs.

14 ounces Abbaye de Belloc cheese, roughly diced

8 ounces Ossau-Iraty cheese, roughly diced

4 ounces feta, crumbled

1 or 2 garlic cloves, halved

1¼ cups vegetable stock

1 to 2 tablespoons cornstarch or all-purpose flour

1 to 2 tablespoon fresh lemon juice

1 small onion, chopped

Freshly ground black pepper

1 teaspoon dried oregano

1. In a medium bowl, combine the three cheeses and toss.

2. Rub the inside of a fondue pot with the garlic clove halves. Add the vegetable stock and heat over medium heat until hot but not boiling. Whisk in the cornstarch, lemon juice, and onion.

3. Add one handful of cheese at a time to the mixture, stirring constantly with a wooden spoon in a figure-eight motion. Wait for each portion of cheese to completely melt before adding the next. Continue stirring until the cheese is completely melted, bubbling gently, and has the appearance of a light creamy sauce.

4. Season with pepper to taste and the dried oregano. Remove the pot from the heat and place over a fondue burner.

Breadzilla

Breadzilla
84 Wainscott NW Road | Wainscott, NY 11975
(631) 537-0955 | www.breadzilla.com

Breadzilla is right next to the Seafood Shop in Wainscott—it's been there for years, but for one reason or another, we never gave it a try. This is a good lesson in looking past your nose and trying everything. Because when we finally did go to Breadzilla, we were surprised and delighted by the quality of the baked goods, the craftsmanship they apply to the art of breadmaking, and the vast selection.

Owners Nancy Hollister and Bradley Thomson use only the best flour and butter in their products. They are perfectionists on a quest to bake the perfect loaf of bread. The Thomsons make everything from scratch based on their own secret recipes and use only local products. They make a truly perfect baguette, crisp on the outside, soft and doughy on the inside. This is no small feat. The East End is tough for breadmaking; the humidity from ocean and bay wreaks havoc on crispness. Breadzilla also offers a wonderful soft white loaf that's perfect for toasting.

At the back of the store you can find jars filled with marvelous biscotti: cherry, cranberry, hazelnut, and more, all definitely worth a try. Another surprise is the outstanding cheese department—don't miss it.

Espresso

Espresso, an Italian takeout market on a side street in Sag Harbor, is one of those places we recommend for just one thing among the many they offer. Although opinions differ about the fare—if you're looking for a good eggplant parmigiano hero sandwich, you can find it here—the hot item at Espresso is the focaccia. They make it daily in their own ovens, and these flatbreads are remarkably flavorful and rich. The crust is baked to crispy perfection, and topped with salt and rosemary. It's perfect with the tuna dip, and what starts out as an appetizer may just end up as the whole meal.

Espresso 184 Division Street | Sag Harbor, NY 11963 | (631) 725-4433

Loaves and Fishes

This pristine and charming prepared foods store occupies a whitewashed wooden shack at the corner of Sagg Main Street and Montauk Highway in Sagaponack. The lobster salad, which rings in at $100 a pound, made the place famous, and as a result, the aggressive, pressed-for-time summer-weekend crowds can overwhelm even the heartiest soul.

But snap judgments are usually unfair, and that goes double for Loaves and Fishes because, in spite of all the blather and hype, the food is superb. True, you may have to take out a second mortgage to make lunch for six, but you can be sure everything will be first rate.

So let's forget the hype and pretend it's a bright midsummer morning.

The first thing you'll notice is a tiny white store, brilliant in the early light. You'll hear the slam and slap of the old-fashioned wooden screen door. There's a bench out front where you can get some sun, eat croissants, and watch the world pass by.

The interior is just as unpretentious. You'll find gray painted-wood floors, white walls, and a long, low glass counter that stretches the length of the narrow store. The counters are filled with Loaves and Fishes unique creations, and what's not homemade comes from only the best sources. The cooking is simple, and the proprietor, Anna Pump, prides herself on using only the freshest, most natural ingredients. The salads are delicious, especially the lobster and chicken, and the savory tarts and dips are definitely worth a try. Loaves and Fishes bakes their own bread every morning, and there's a tempting selection of freshly baked pastries and cakes as well. The refrigerator is stocked with a variety of soups, including a white gazpacho with grapes that is one of our favorites.

Loaves and Fishes offers everything you need to prepare lunch for as few as two people or as many as twenty. Pick up a fresh baguette, hummus, and a lemon bar, and you've got the makings of a great beach picnic.

Loaves and Fishes 50 Sagg Main Street | Sagaponack, NY 11962 | (631) 537-0555 | www.landfcookshop.com

SUMMER BERRY CREAM TART

Serves 6 to 8

Anna Pump created this tart recipe especially for this book. It's a great showcase for local fruit. The tart is best the day it is made.

CRUST

1¼ cups all-purpose flour

⅓ cup cocoa powder

⅓ cup sugar

1 teaspoon vanilla extract

¼ teaspoon salt

6 ounces cold butter, cut into ½-inch slices

¼ cup water

FILLING

6 ounces cream cheese

½ cup sour cream

2 teaspoons lemon juice

½ teaspoon vanilla extract

½ cup superfine sugar

1¾ cups fresh raspberries

1¾ cups fresh blueberries

⅓ cup seedless raspberry jam

1. Butter a 9-inch tart pan with a removable bottom.

2. **Prepare the crust:** Combine the first five ingredients in the bowl of a food processor. Add the butter and pulse until the mixture resembles coarse meal. Continue processing while slowly adding the water; process until the dough forms clumps. Transfer the dough to a work table and gather it into a ball. Chill for about 30 minutes.

3. On a lightly floured surface, roll out the dough to a 13-inch round. Transfer to the tart pan, pressing firmly and fluting the edges. Trim the excess.

4. Freeze the crust for at least 1 hour. Preheat the oven to 375 degrees F. Remove the crust from the freezer and bake 25 to 30 minutes. Allow to cool completely.

5. **Prepare the filling:** Combine the first five ingredients in the bowl of an electric mixer and blend at medium speed until smooth. Spread the filling over the crust and scatter the berries over the top. Warm the jam with a tablespoon of water until smooth; brush over the berries.

Pike Farm

You'll find Pike's Farm Stand on Sagg Main Street—a charming village roadway with one of the state's last one-room schoolhouses, a working farm, and a tiny general store.

Just about all the vegetables and berries for sale at this little farm stand on Sagg Main Street in Sagaponack are grown on the tiny 7.5-acre plot directly behind the retail carts.

The Pikes offer a stunning array of fresh fruits and vegetables, but the tomatoes just might be the best in the world, at least according to locals, who aren't really locals at all but world travelers. They can be seen on any given summer day stuffing their precious tomatoes into brown paper bags.

And it's true, these tomatoes are supernatural. Maybe it's the soil, the seeds, or the way they cultivate their vegetables, but there's nothing like the taste of a ripe sun-warmed Pike's beefsteak sliced and dripping juice, sprinkled with a little sea salt. It's heaven.

Pike Farm Sagg Main Street | Sagaponack, NY 11962 | (631) 537-5854

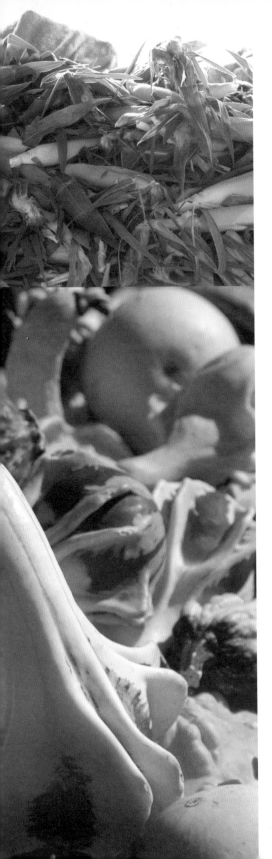

BLACKBERRY SLUMP

Serves 4 to 6

This is an easy recipe for a big summer crowd, and best of all, it can be whipped up at the last minute. It was contributed by Jennifer Pike.

4 cups fresh blackberries

1 cup sugar

1 cup all-purpose flour

1½ teaspoons baking powder

¼ teaspoon salt

¾ cup whole milk

2 tablespoons unsalted butter, melted

1. Preheat the oven to 375 degrees F.

2. Put the berries in an ungreased 5- to 6-cup gratin dish and sprinkle evenly with ¾ cup of the sugar.

3. In a mixing bowl, sift together the flour, baking powder, salt, and remaining ¼ cup sugar. Add the milk and butter and whisk until smooth.

4. Pour the mixture over the berries (they may not be completely covered). Bake until the top is golden, 40 to 45 minutes. Cool for 20 minutes and serve warm.

Foster Farm

Marilee Foster, who writes a regular column for the *Southampton Press*, runs one of the finest and tiniest farm stands anywhere in the East. It's an unmanned drive-up, and shoppers pay for their vegetables by tucking more or less the exact change into a too-small slot cut into a rusting metal box that sits neatly next to the asparagus. It's unclear whether the box is bolted down, but Marilee says she seldom comes up short. The stand is all of three feet wide and six feet tall, but Marilee's vegetables are legendary—and in extremely short supply. The asparagus usually disappears within a half hour.

In the height of the season, Marilee may put out a second bunch in the afternoon, but most days the stand is sold out by noon. It's up to the buyer to know the growing seasons and to get there early.

Foster Farm
729 Sagg Main Road | Sagaponack, NY 11962 | (631) 537-0700

TOMATO JAM

The tomato has become one of the most popular vegetable crops on Long Island, and you will find it in almost every farm stand. Some of the best are from the Lee Foster Farm in Sagaponack.

---

1 cup sugar

1½ pounds ripe tomatoes, peeled and chopped

2 tablespoons fresh lime juice

1 tablespoon chopped fresh ginger

⅛ teaspoon ground cloves

1 teaspoon salt

1 small jalapeño pepper, stemmed, seeded, and minced

Freshly ground white pepper to taste

---

1. Combine all the ingredients in a medium saucepan. Bring to a boil over medium heat, stirring often.

2. Reduce the heat and simmer, stirring occasionally, until the mixture has the consistency of thick jam, about 1 hour and 20 minutes. Season to taste.

3. Let cool and refrigerate until ready to use. You may keep it for a few days in the refrigerator or freeze.

Lisa and Bill's Farm Stand

Wainscott's Main Street runs one mile from Town Line Lane to the private entrance of the Georgica Association, and it is one of the most beautiful stretches on the East End. You'll see working barns, with wrecked cars on blocks, next to painstakingly restored colonial homes, a tiny school, and an even tinier community house. Along the south side is an enormous preserve of wildflowers, marsh grass, and pond that extends about a mile until it reaches the ocean dunes.

Here, on the corner of Beach Lane, you'll find Lisa and Bill Babinski's farm stand, which is really just a cart on truck tires. The Babinskis grow all their produce on the few acres that stretch south behind the stand. The brother-and-sister team has been at this location since 1992, but the Babinski family has been farming on the East End since the early 1800s. Their mother, Lisa, works the stand and knows just about everyone by their first names. During the summer, the Babinskis grow tomatoes, zucchini, cucumbers, string beans, snap peas, eggplant, onions, asparagus, potatoes, strawberries, and melons, and in the fall their field is covered with bright orange pumpkins.

The produce here is very good, all organic, changing with the seasons. The best time to come may be the fall, when you can take the kids out into the pumpkin patch to pick their own Halloween pumpkin.

Lisa and Bill's Farm Stand
Main Street and Beach Lane | Wainscott, NY 11975

CORN PUDDING

Serves 4 to 6

Corn pudding is a year-round favorite—Long Island corn has a very sweet taste—but in the summertime, when corn is so abundant, it is perfect with just about anything. It's delicious on its own, too, served with fish, chicken, or a mixed salad and a good bottle of white wine. As the song goes, the "corn is as high as an elephant's eye and reaching right up to the sky."

---

4 tablespoons (½ stick) unsalted butter

2 eggs

2 teaspoons kosher salt or sea salt

2 tablespoons sugar

½ teaspoon freshly ground pepper

2 cups milk

½ cup all-purpose flour

2½ cups fresh corn off the cob (from about 4 ears)

---

1. Preheat the oven to 350 degrees F.

2. Place the butter in a 9-by-13-inch casserole and melt it in the oven.

3. In a medium bowl, beat together the eggs, salt, sugar, pepper, milk, and flour. When the mixture is smooth, stir in the corn.

4. Remove the casserole dish from the oven and pour the butter into the corn mixture, stirring to mix. Pour the corn mixture back into the casserole and bake for 1 hour, or until the mixture has set and is browned on top.

Iacono Farm

This old-school, family-run chicken farm on Long Lane, just outside the village of East Hampton, produces and sells the best chicken west of Brest, but it is not a place for the faint of heart. The chickens are truly free range. They're all over the place, and they are slaughtered on demand, in full view, in the back of the Iacono's barnlike retail building.

Salvatore Iacono, who managed the farm for some forty years, died in 2008. But thanks to his wife, Eileen, and their son Anthony, the place is still world class. Eileen runs the retail operation, and Anthony handles the poultry.

The chickens are not certified organic by current definition, but they have plenty of space to graze and are not fed hormones or antibiotics. You can buy a whole bird or pieces; the capon is especially good. (For taste, two capons beat one turkey anytime.) If you buy chicken cut into pieces, make sure to ask for the feet; add them to stock to thicken soup.

The Iaconos also sell delicious fresh hen's eggs, in various sizes, either white or brown. And unlike the store-bought variety, these fresh eggs do not require immediate refrigeration.

Iacono Farm 106 Long Lane | East Hampton, NY 11937 | (631) 324-1107

The Seafood Shop

Shopping at the Seafood Shop on a Saturday in August is the closest you'll come to roller derby in the Hamptons. Buying fish here in summer is a contact sport.

Located on Montauk Highway in Wainscott, this little shop attracts fish lovers from Bridgehampton to East Hampton, and in summer that's a crowd. Lines usually stretch out the door, wending around the lobster tanks to the big glass fish counter at the rear. A lot of humanity is packed into a small space in search of the ocean's bounty. For the most part, the spirit is friendly, with line-mates waiting patiently; but occasionally some fool tries to jump the line and then all hell breaks loose. It's like swimming into a school of ravenous bluefish.

A few very good reasons account for the crowds. First, the Seafood Shop is one of the very best fish purveyors on the East End. The fish and shellfish are first-class and mostly local, purchased directly—whenever possible—from nearby fisheries. They make their own outstanding soups; the Manhattan and New England clam or fish chowders make a memorable winter meal. Second, the service is impeccable and consistent, and the same staff works the counters year after year. Their advice is superb; they recommend whole fish over fillets for flavor and cooking shrimp in the shell, and their recipe for sautéing scallops is one of the tried and true. If you need even more insider advice, the *Seafood Shop Cookbook* is full of imaginative ways to prepare their offerings.

The Seafood Shop 356 Montauk Highway | Wainscott, NY 11975
(631) 537-0633 | www.theseafoodshop.com

DEBBIE'S BROILED BLUEFISH

Serves 5 to 6

One of the most popular game fish along the coast of Long Island is bluefish. Usually traveling in large schools in the Atlantic Ocean, they range from Nova Scotia to the southern tip of South America. They are named for their greenish blue to silver coloring. The smaller ones are called "snappers" and are the best for eating. These are usually 2 to 4 pounds.

2 pounds bluefish fillets, about 1-inch thick

Salt and freshly ground pepper

¼ cup mayonnaise

Paprika

Lemon wedges

1. Preheat the broiler; wash and pat dry the fillets.

2. Sprinkle both sides of each fillet with salt and pepper to taste. Liberally spread each fillet with mayonnaise and then sprinkle with paprika.

3. Place the fillets in a greased broiler pan. Broil 3 to 5 inches from the heat for 8 to 10 minutes. For fillets thicker than 1 inch, turn and broil another 5 to 8 minutes. Serve immediately, with lemon wedges.

EECO Farm

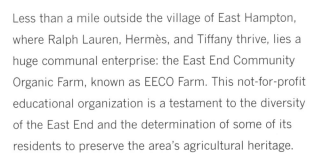

Less than a mile outside the village of East Hampton, where Ralph Lauren, Hermès, and Tiffany thrive, lies a huge communal enterprise: the East End Community Organic Farm, known as EECO Farm. This not-for-profit educational organization is a testament to the diversity of the East End and the determination of some of its residents to preserve the area's agricultural heritage.

The site is beautiful, with long furrows stretching across acres of flat open fields. In the evenings, it looks more like Iowa than Long Island. The EECO Farm is open to community participation, and anyone willing and able can join for a nominal fee, help cultivate the crops, and share in the harvest.

We found this eloquent list of objectives in the farm's mission statement:

"Grow fresh vegetables for the community
Give children their first farming experience
Train and employ local youth in agriculture
Encourage mentoring between generations
Add organic crop farming to everyday life
Work with religious, social, and service groups
Develop educational programs for the public
Provide sustainable gardening information
Encourage responsible stewardship of the land."

EECO Farm 55 Long Lane | East Hampton, NY 11937
(631) 329-4694 | www.eecofarm.org

Claws on Wheels

The Puritans thrived on hard work, so it's no surprise that making the traditional New England clambake entails hours of backbreaking work: digging a five-foot-deep pit on the beach; heating heavy stones in an open fire and then placing them at the bottom of the pit; sandwiching lobsters, clams, mussels, chicken, and sometimes sausage between layers of wet seaweed all the way to the top of the pit; covering the whole thing with canvas or potato sacks soaked in seawater; and, finally, letting it all steam for eight to twelve hours. The results are incredibly delicious.

But why take all that time, why do all that work, when you can get Michael Bunce, owner of Claws on Wheels, to do it for you?

Michael's company creates and serves custom clambakes up and down the Hamptons' beaches. They will handle anything, from a small family picnic to dinner for two hundred, complete with linen tablecloths, fine china, and quality stemware. The retail store offers all the stuff that clambakes are made of, plus an excellent fish market and a fine selection of prepared foods.

They make all the prepared foods in the store, where you'll find some unique twists on traditional fare. The guacamole with hand-cut plantain chips is sumptuous. The seaweed salad, lentil salad, tortilla chips, tuna salad, clam chowder, coleslaw, cedar plank salmon—all created by Michael and his executive chef—are unusual, delicious, and memorable.

Claws on Wheels 17 Race Lane | East Hampton, NY 11937
(631) 324-9224 | www.clawsonwheels.net

Villa Italian Food

When Villa Italian Specialties opened across from the East Hampton train station more than twenty years ago, it was the first in the area to make sausage on the premises. And from day one, the store has had an enormous local following.

Villa makes the best sausage on the East End. It's that simple. They make them by hand, from their own recipes, with dozens of different types to suit every taste. When you look through the pristine glass displays, you'll likely be boggled by the choices, but don't worry. You can't make a bad one.

The chefs at Villa also make pickled tripe, superior meatballs, and a huge selection of salami. The salads, olives, eggplant caponata, and pickled vegetables are always fresh and full of surprising flavor. The hero sandwiches are legendary, as attested by the lunchtime lines of local workers stretching out onto North Main Street. A barbecue with Villa sausages, roasted peppers, and onions is a summer highlight.

Villa Italian Food 7 Railroad Avenue | East Hampton, NY 11937 | (631) 324-5110 | www.villaitalianspecialties.com

Dreesen's Donuts

Back in the early 70s it used to be possible to buy bait at a store called Tony's Tackle on Newtown Lane in East Hampton. These days on the same street you can only find supplies for social trolling, at stores like Scoop, Calypso, or Tory Burch.

One of the last holdouts from the old days was Dreesen's, a small grocer with one of the best butcher shops anywhere in the United States.

Dreesen's closed about five years ago, but one remnant of their business keeps chugging along: the stainless-steel donut machine that entertained generations of East End kids who stopped to watch the beautiful golden donuts work their way down the conveyor belt. The machine is still in the window, and the corner of the current store it occupies is called Dreesen's Donuts. The donuts are still wonderful. Stop in and buy a dozen.

Dreesen's Donuts 33 Newton Lane | East Hampton, NY 11937 | (631) 324-0465

Lucy's Whey

East Hampton's Main Street was once the epitome of "Main Street America"—home to a five-and-dime, pharmacy, toy store, donut store, butcher, bait shop, and gas station. Today it overflows with high-end global logos like Ralph Lauren, Tiffany, and Louis Vuitton. Yet one can still find in spaces too small for big names some wonderful, new, on-a-shoestring food stores. One of these is Lucy's Whey, squeezed into a former barbershop in an alley off North Main Street.

The store could be renamed Lucy's Cheese School, for owners Catherine Bodziner and Lucy Kazickas are dedicated to educating Americans about the cheeses that are made right in their own backyards. Although the phrase *American cheese* may conjure images of tasteless yellow squares, let the proprietors at Lucy's Cheese show you otherwise. They've gotten to know artisanal cheese makers throughout the country, and everything offered in their shop—from the olive oils to the chutneys—is American made.

Lucy's Whey 80 North Main Street | East Hampton, NY 11937
(631) 324-4428 | www.lucyswhey.com

Round Swamp Farm

TRUFFLE OIL MAYONNAISE WITH GREEN ASPARAGUS

Serves 4

Start this recipe at the beginning of the asparagus season and do not stop until early winter. Also try this recipe with tomatoes, cauliflower, or carrots. It can be used as a sauce for an appetizer or for dipping with cocktails.

---

2 egg whites

1 cup mayonnaise

⅓ cup truffle oil

Salt and pepper

1 bunch asparagus

Last year, we were invited for a Sunday lunch at a friend's, and when I mentioned how much I enjoyed the food, my friend proudly told me that it all came from the Round Swamp Farm stand. In France we make lunch for friends; in the Hamptons, people buy it, ready-made, and bring it home to serve. It took me a while to get used to this custom, but the food from Round Swamp was so good, I've since become a convert.

For me Round Swamp was a discovery; for the rest of the Hamptons, it's an institution. The Snyder family has been running the farm stand at the same location for four generations.

This place has everything. You could put together a month of lunches and not repeat yourself—great fruits and vegetables, prepared foods, desserts. Among our favorites: Claire's Lemon Pound Cake, Shelley's Ginger Green Tea, raspberry/cherry crumb cake, and Lisa's Brownie Bites. The blueberries and strawberries are succulent in season, and all the vegetables are grown on the Snyders' twenty-acre farm. There's even entertainment for the kids in the form of rabbits and chickens.

Round Swamp Farm 184 Three Mile Harbor Road | East Hampton, NY 11937 | (631) 324-4438 | www.roundswampfarm.com

1. With an electric mixer, whisk the egg whites in a mixing bowl until soft peaks form. Reduce the mixer to slow speed, then add the mayonnaise and truffle oil. Season with salt and pepper to taste. Cover the sauce with plastic wrap (to avoid discoloration) and place it in the refrigerator for at least 2 hours.

2. Clean the asparagus under cold water; trim and peel from tip to top. Steam the spears in a steamer for about 10 minutes, or until fork-tender. Allow to cool to room temperature (it tastes better that way).

3. Arrange the spears on a tray, accompanied by the mayonnaise in a bowl.

Dear Charlotte:
Thank you so much for showing us around the fish market! We had a lot of fun learning about the lobsters. It was cool watching you clean the striped bass. You made it look easy!
Thank you for the porgies. We had fun making fish prints. As you can see, they looked really neat!
Thank you, thank you!
Amagansett School Pre-K 3
+ Mrs. Bianchi
March 2006

PLease Do Not Touch THE LOBSTERS.
THANK YOU

Stuart's Seafood Market

Peter Matthiessen's recently reissued book *Men's Lives* tells the story of the haul-seine fishermen of Amagansett and Springs. They were called Bonackers, after Accabonac Harbor in Springs, and some spoke a dialect that could be traced back to speech patterns of seventeenth-century Dorset.

The families remain, but the old ways have slowly died out. Size limits on striped bass put an end to haul-seining, and the once-bountiful scallop harvest in Gardiners Bay is all but gone.

But Stuart's Seafood Market, almost hidden off Route 27 on tiny Oak Lane in Amagansett, continues to thrive. Established in 1955 by Stuart Vorpahl, a bay man, Stuart's was originally the place the haul-seiners brought their catch for icing and shipment to Fulton Fish Market. The retail shop was an afterthought, but it became increasingly popular with locals and the summer people who had begun to take over the area. The store changed ownership in 1997, but the local spirit still imbues the place, as evoked by testimonials from well-known residents that cover the walls.

Stuart's has since added a catering business, specializing in clambakes, barbecues, and pig roasts. They still buy local catch, supplemented by trips to Fulton Fish Market and direct shipments from around the world. Their lobster rolls are up there on the all-time-greats list, and be sure to try the salmon candy and key lime pie to finish off your perfect fish dinner.

Stuart's Seafood Market 41 Oak Lane | Amagansett, NY 11930
(631) 267-6700 | www.stuartsseafood.com

LOBSTER CAKE

Serves 4

Stuart's Seafood Market makes great lobster cakes for purchase, but here's a recipe if you want to try making them yourself. All the ingredients can be purchased at the store. Serve as an appetizer or with a green salad.

4 tablespoons butter

3 scallions, chopped

½ red bell pepper, cored, seeded, and chopped

1 pound precooked lobster meat, chopped

1½ teaspoons Dijon mustard

½ cup mayonnaise

1 egg, beaten

1 tablespoon chopped parsley

1½ cups panko breadcrumbs

1. Heat 1 tablespoon of the butter in a saucepan and sauté the scallions and bell pepper until the pepper begins to soften.

2. In a large bowl, combine the lobster, Dijon mustard, mayonnaise, egg, and parsley with the scallion and bell pepper. Refrigerate for 1 hour.

3. Remove from the refrigerator. Shape the lobster mixture into cakes about the size of a walnut and flatten and roll them in the panko breadcrumbs.

4. In a large skillet over medium heat, sauté the cakes in remaining butter 3 to 4 minutes until golden.

Tutto Italiano

The Red Horse Plaza is a chic little shopping triangle made up of antiques stores, an exclusive spa, and an upscale wine shop. But, in a typical bit of Hamptonian cultural dissonance, at Tutto Italiano, in this same little square, Friday and Saturday mornings, you can watch chef Pasquale Langella, red-faced and grunting over a steaming pot of boiled curds, as he makes world-class mozzarella by hand, one piece at a time.

Tutto Italiano is part of the Citarella group of gourmet grocers, and, true to its name, it carries only Italian specialties. Tutto was moderately successful from the beginning, offering homemade pasta, a varied selection of cheeses, and select cold cuts, but what put it over the top was the mozzarella. Maybe they have some secret ingredient, or maybe it's the way Langella handles the curds, but everyone who tries this mozzarella agrees it's the best you can find this side of Naples. But be warned, if you want to try it, you'd better show up very early; it's always sold out before noon.

Fortunately for latecomers, Langella also uses his mozzarella to make crusty individual pizzas, and he turns out first-rate focaccia in the same brick oven. Tutto Italiano offers rich full-flavored cappuccino, a huge selection of olive oils, and, according to one Italian friend, the best veal meatballs on Long Island.

All the ingredients for antipasto are prime: mushrooms, roasted red peppers, artichoke hearts, and prosciutto. Drizzle a little oil on some freshly toasted focaccia, top it with a roasted pepper and maybe an anchovy, and . . . *tutto bene.*

Tutto Italiano 74 Montauk Highway | East Hampton, NY 11937 | (631) 324-9500

RHONE

Amagansett Village Wine and Spirits

Along with the burgeoning wine-making business on Long Island, a few world-class wine shops have emerged on the East End. One of the best is Amagansett Village Wine and Spirits. Amagansett is miles away from the nearest vineyard, and although Village Wine carries a selection of local varietals, it is the unusually deep and well-researched choice of wines from around the world that make this store special.

The chances are good that no matter how knowledgeable you are about wine, you'll discover a couple of great bottles you've never heard of. Their collection of first-rate Spanish wines is dazzling. All the greats are covered, many in hard-to-get vintages. But the fun here is letting the expert salespeople guide you to something new.

Amagansett Village Wine and Spirits 203 Main Street
Amagansett, NY 11930 | (631) 267-3939 | www.amagansettwine.net

Mary's Marvelous

This quaint café and bakery in the charming village of Amagansett is a great place to take a break from the ordeal of rifling through the village's many outstanding antiques stores. (Two of the best such shops are Balasses, which carries an eclectic mix of antiques and fine reproductions, all set in a beautiful old house and three barns; and Nellie's, specializing in early-American primitive antiques and crafts. Both are worth a stop.)

Everything at Mary's is homemade. The shortbread is about the best anywhere, made from unbleached flour, butter, sugar, and salt. She also makes a wonderfully nutty granola. The sandwiches are hearty and simple. Everyone makes egg salad, but Mary's version is just marvelous.

Mary's Marvelous 209 Main Street | Amagansett, NY 11930 | (631) 267-8796
www.marysmarvelous.com

Hampton Chutney

Amagansett Farmers Market

Many have traveled to India in search of spiritual enlightenment. But Gary MacGurn, the proprietor of Hampton Chutney, hit the subcontinental jackpot. He probably did find enlightenment there, but more important, he also met his wife, Isabel, and came back with a mission that he would turn into a thriving business. The mission: to introduce Americans to the joys of chutneys and dosas.

After working five years in the kitchen of an ashram, Gary developed a flair for making chutney, which became the first offering of his newly opened Hampton Chutney. His piquant condiments are less spicy than their Indian counterparts—adjusted for American tastes—but they are just as delicious and still pack some wallop. Particular favorites are the cilantro, peanut, and mango varieties.

After their initial success with chutney, the couple started making dosas, crêpes made on an open griddle from a batter of lentils and rice. At Hampton Chutney, the dosas are filled with tomatoes, avocado, spinach, potatoes—whatever you choose from the long list on the menu—and then slathered with your favorite chutney. The results are delicious and surprisingly light.

To create your own bliss, take your favorite stuffed dosa wrapped in paper to one of the picnic tables outside the store and enjoy it accompanied by a lilting sitar raga.

The village of Amagansett has always been a bit of an outlier. Located three miles east of East Hampton, the hamlet affects an un-Hamptonian earthy air, though hidden behind the hedges of Further Lane are some of the biggest estates on the East End. These stately properties run from the road to the double dunes that line Amagansett's beautiful ocean beaches.

One of the set pieces of this un-Hampton was the Amagansett Farmers Market, started by Pat Struk in 1954. A ramshackle collection of shacks and stands, the market managed to convey a pleasing bohemian ethos in spite of escalating prices and more and more sophisticated prepared foods.

Then, two years ago, Struk sold the property to Eli Zabar, and the village was up in arms (well, as up in arms as a laid-back place like Amagansett can get). Villagers imagined a Vinegar Factory East, but they need not have worried. Under Zabar's keen eye, the Amagansett Farmers Market looks even more authentic, more laid-back than it did before.

Always an enjoyable stop, either for lunch at the roadside tables or for picking up ingredients for your next meal, the new and improved market is still a must on any trip along Route 27.

Hampton Chutney   Amagansett Square on Main Street
Amagansett, NY 11937 | (631) 267-3131 | www.hamptonchutney.com

Amagansett Farmers Market   367 Main Street
Amagansett, NY 11930 | (631) 267-3894 | www.elizabar.com

Quail Hill Farm

The manager of Quail Hill, a cooperative farm established on land donated for the purpose, hands out business cards that read "Scott Chaskey—Poet, Farmer," and he does indeed look like Walt Whitman (or Santa Claus).

Chaskey is a warm and kind man who clearly takes deep emotional pleasure from farming. He exudes a sense of peace and tranquility. Chaskey's goal is to "sustain the land in a healthy condition for future generations." He is the author of *The Common Ground: Seasons on an Organic Farm*, a book that sets out the need to realize his business card's claim. In it, he mixes poetic observation with practical advice on farming. As he explains, "I have learned to cultivate crops and poetic meter, but wild nature is a parent to each."

Quail Hill is a truly cooperative farm. Members work the land under Scott's supervision, supplying more than two hundred local families as well as several nearby schools, restaurants, and food pantries with fresh, healthy produce.

The work is arduous. A photographer friend, Jerome Albertini, decided to take a year off to work at the farm, and this is what he says about the experience: "It is quite busy and physical every day, rain or shine, hot or cold, all this since mid-March. It involves seeding, greenhousing, watering, planting, weeding, cultivating, wheel-hoeing, hoeing manually, thinning, mulching, composting, tractoring, harvesting, cleaning, selling, preparing, trellising, pruning . . . every single thing you can think of and all without any big machines (a few old tractors), mostly by hand. I am in perfect shape and in total fusion between my mind and Nature."

Quail Hill Farm 660 Old Stone Highway | Amagansett, NY 11930
(631) 267-8492 | www.peconiclandtrust.org/quail_hill_farm

WHITE GARLIC SOUP

Serves 5

We first tried this recipe in New York City in the middle of winter at our friend Imma's home; she had just delivered her second baby but still found the time to prepare a fantastic Spanish meal, starting with this Ajo Blanco Soup, a recipe from Andalusia. Now we enjoy it on Long Island with fresh local young garlic.

½ cup blanched almonds

2 young fresh garlic cloves

½ cup cubed white bread (with crust discarded)

2 cups olive oil, plus more for serving

2 cups water

Salt and freshly ground white pepper

1. In a blender, process together the almonds, garlic, and bread until finely ground. While still processing, slowly add the olive oil until smooth; then pour in the water. The consistency should be very liquid; add more water if necessary. Season with salt and white pepper to taste.

2. Transfer to a bowl and chill in the refrigerator for 3 hours. Serve in individual bowls, garnished with a drizzle of olive oil.

Multi Aquaculture Systems Inc.

A magnificent stretch of dune runs nearly seven miles from the eastern edge of Amagansett to the Hither Hills State Park at Montauk. The entire dune, ranging from the Atlantic Ocean to Gardiners Bay, was formerly owned by the Smith Fish Meal Company, whose fleet dragged the bay for moss bunker that they converted into fertilizer in their beachside furnaces. The process was notoriously smelly. At the turn of the last century, a well-to-do Midwestern family bought a huge tract of land, sight unseen, and unfortunately downwind from the fertilizer factory, and then built a series of mansions for their many members. They arrived one August, spent two nights, and quickly fled back to Ohio, never to return. A clear victory for the moss bunkers. The massive estates stayed empty for years.

The fertilizer company is long gone, and today the Napeague stretch is one of the wildest, most beautiful places on Long Island. Ospreys nest all around, herons wade the inlets, cranberries grow wild in the dunes. In season, one can harvest them, along with wild beach plums and bayberries. On the part of the dune called Promised Land stands a series of rusting, corrugated steel structures that look like a movie set but were actually part of a failed government project to stimulate the fishing industry. The decrepit buildings stood vacant for years until Marie and Bob Valenti decided to open their aquaculture business there.

The Valentis manage Multi Aquaculture Systems Inc., an ecologically sound fish-farming operation, and they are extremely protective of the environment. Marie and Bob started their business hoping to replenish the then-diminished striped bass population, but today they raise several species of fish in their huge tanks and farm lobster as well. Much of their product is sold to fish markets around the world.

Tucked among this surreal bayside enclave of rusted steel and giant concrete fish tanks is a little shop that looks like a direct transplant from Provence.

Multi Aquaculture Systems Inc. 429 Cranberry Hole Road | Amagansett, NY 11930 | (631) 267-3341

FISH · FARM

LOBSTER
SEAFOOD

MULTI

AQUACULTU

SYSTEMS

429

The shop, variously called the Fish Farm or the Fish Factory, is run by a transplanted Provençale who sells prepared foods and serves lunch. Her name is Nadine and she runs the store for the Valentis. Everything is made on demand in the small kitchen behind the shop: lobster rolls, lobster soup with tequila, pissaladière. Nadine makes an incredible tarte tatin and Paris-Brest pastry. You can also find products from small French producers. (I recommend the lemon preserves.) There is of course a small but impeccable fresh fish department, too, with live lobsters, mussels, and oysters.

Have lunch at one of the picnic tables and then go for a long stroll on the Gardiners Bay beach. This is a perfect place for really fresh fish and homemade produce, and don't forget to bring your own bottle of wine. In the fall, you can just cross the road and pick your own cranberries.

Bon Bons Chocolatier

This family business, located on charming Main Street in Huntington Village, is chocolate heaven. From the beautifully designed store to the vast glass-walled kitchen to the spectacular selection, everything about Bon Bons Chocolatier exudes quality, craftsmanship, and a passion for chocolate. Mary Alice Meinersman started the business in 1989 with her late husband and now runs it with her daughter Susanna. In 1992, head candymaker Eric Lobignat arrived directly from a great chocolatier on the Rue François Ler in Paris. He loves life in the United States, and his skilled hand adds a special grace to these chocolates.

The front of the store changes seasonally, like a movie set for chocolate. Just open the door, and the heady chocolate aroma surrounds you. The selection is large and very good. They carry more than forty varieties of fudge, and if you show up early enough you can see them making it in the open kitchen. Watch as they mix crème fraîche and sugar—the beginnings of great fudge—in a warm copper pot.

It would take several days to try everything in the store, but you can't go wrong with the amazing fudge, marshmallows, and milk minis. They also offer jelly beans, fresh and delicious in more flavors than you can imagine. This is a great place for a family excursion.

Bon Bons Chocolatier 319 Main Street | Huntington, NY 11743
(631) 549-1059 | www.bonbonschocolatier.com

Miloski's Poultry Farm

If, while driving along Route 25 in Suffolk County, you are overcome by an overwhelming hunger for yak meat, don't fret. You can satiate your appetite at Will Miloski's Poultry Farm, along with your desire for rattlesnake, crocodile, kangaroo, wild boar, and frog's legs. The freezer at Miloski's is full of exotic meats from all over the world, but what the place is really about is delicious poultry raised right there on the farm.

The chicken is free range, properly fed, and delicious, as is the turkey, duck, goose, squab, and pheasant. A special treat is the capon, a richer, fuller-tasting type of chicken.

Long Island families have been buying their Thanksgiving turkeys at Miloski's since the farm opened in 1946. And once you taste one of these birds for yourself, you'll understand why.

**Miloski's
Poultry Farm**

4418 Middle Country Road
Calverton, NY 11933
(631) 727-0239

North Quarter Farm

North Quarter Farm
Roanoke Avenue | Riverhead, NY
11901 | (516) 647-1146

Ed Tuccio and Dee Muma put an interesting spin on the locavore movement. They breed American bison in Riverhead, New York, which means that Long Islanders can now—after 10,000 years of doing without—enjoy locally raised bison meat, lean, low in cholesterol, and naturally sweet. The North Quarter herd of more than a thousand grazes on three hundred acres of prairie grass—a truly inspiring sight. These animals are majestic, almost mythic looking, and apparently quite dangerous, which explains the high and heavy fence. The animals thrive on a diet of local grass, Canadian hay, and corn, all grown organically and without hormones.

Bison, commonly known as buffalo, were once abundant on the American prairie. Today their range is extremely restricted, making their appearance particularly special in this part of southeastern New York. Brought back from near extinction a century ago, the American bison now faces a brighter future, thanks to dedicated ranchers such as North Quarter Farm.

Briermere Farm

The Briermere family's century-old white clapboard farmhouse would not look out of place alongside a state highway in rural Iowa. Once inside the house you'll see rough wooden shelves piled high with baked goods—pies, breads, jams, and cookies, all of it made right there on the farm by the Briermeres. They jar all the jellies and jams on the premises, then set them out in alphabetical order, from apricot to strawberry, with sixteen flavors in between. Neatness counts, but the real test is in the taste, and these jams and jellies are remarkable. They retain the essence of the fruit without adding much else to obscure the subtle flavors. Spread on a slice of Briermere bread, lightly toasted and buttered, they are heaven.

Briermere tarts are incredible, too—rhubarb in spring, raspberry peach for summer, and apple in fall, with many more flavors to choose from. Be sure to try the blueberry muffins, filled to bursting with fruits picked fresh.

The Briermeres use only local ingredients and their own family recipes. This is a wonderful place to spend a few hours in America's rural past.

Briermere Farm 4414 Sound Avenue | Riverhead, NY 11901
(631) 722-3931 | www.briermere.com

Garden of Eve

Eve and Chris Kaplan-Walbrecht started this delightful farm at the turn of the new century and decided to go completely organic. That is no easy task; it's one thing to say your farm is organic but another thing entirely to be certified by the federal government. That means every practice on the farm must meet stringent U.S. Department of Agriculture requirements.

Eve and Chris's hard work and dedication show in the quality of the produce they sell. The vegetables are deeply flavorful, and the eggs have the orange yolk that only the best eggs have. In the barn next to the farm stand, you'll find piglets, Nigerian Dwarf goats, Rhode Island Red chickens, and Border Leicester sheep. This menagerie is part of the micro-ecosystem created by the Kaplan-Walbrechts to ensure that their farm remains organic. Organic farming is labor intensive, with much lower yields per acre than chemical farming, so Garden of Eve requires a lot of support from people who believe in sustainable, ecologically sound farming. So make sure you don't miss this one. And if you would like to learn firsthand how to cultivate your own produce organically, you can volunteer to work on the farm during the summer months.

Garden of Eve 4558 Sound Avenue | Riverhead, NY 11901 | (631) 680-1699
www.gardenofevefarm.com

Crescent Duck Farm

If you take Route 24 south from Riverhead toward Hampton Bays, you will pass the Giant Duck. Made from concrete and plaster, this 1930s icon is an artifact of Long Island's historic association with the Pekin duck. At one time more than sixty million ducks lived on farms all along the island, and Long Island duck was as commonplace as Maine Lobster, but it's no longer so easy to find a duck farm on Long Island. As suburban communities encroached on farmland and the U.S. Environmental Protection Agency started to enforce stricter pollution standards— if unmanaged, the ducks release high concentrations of E. coli into the ecosystem—the farms began to disappear so that now only a few remain.

Crescent Duck Farm, located at the end of an inlet in Peconic Bay, is one of the survivors. It's run by the fifth generation of the Gorwin family, and the founder's descendants have devoted their lives to the business, meeting stringent antipollution standards required by local, state, and federal agencies.

For taste and tenderness, the Long Island duck is still unmatched, and the Gorwin family provides the highest quality available anywhere. Their birds are raised free range and delivered fresh. At Crescent Duck, visitors will witness a fast-disappearing part of Long Island's agricultural history.

Crescent Duck Farm
P.O. Box 500 | Aquebogue, NY 11931 | (631) 722-8000

CRISPY ROAST LONG ISLAND DUCK

Serves 4

John Ross is one of the most acclaimed chefs on the North Fork; he was a restaurant owner for thirty years and wrote several books on using local ingredients. This is one of his recipes. Eric Fry says that with duck there is only one choice of wine: pinot!

1 (6-pound) Long Island duck

1 onion, quartered

Salt

⅓ cup honey

1. Preheat the oven to 500 degrees F.

2. Prepare the duck: Remove the giblets and neck from the cavity and rinse the body under cold water. Cut off the tail, flap of neck skin, and wing tips. Place the onion and salt to taste into the cavity. Push the legs up against the breast and tie with butcher's twine; tie the wings against the body. Puncture the duck skin all over with a fork, brush with the honey, and season with salt.

3. Place the duck on its side on a rack in a shallow roasting pan. Bake for about 20 minutes, or until lightly browned.

4. Reduce the oven temperature to 425 degrees and turn the duck breast-side up. Cover loosely with foil and bake for another 1½ hours. The duck will become very crisp and brown as the honey caramelizes. Remove from the oven and cool to room temperature.

5. Using a chef's knife, split the duck in half and remove the backbone. Using your fingers, remove the rib bones and cartilage. Twist out the thigh bone. Reheat the duck briefly in a hot oven before serving.

Bayview Farm Market

Route 25 runs from Riverhead to Orient Point, and though it is best known for its vineyards, you can find some excellent farm stands along the road. Two of the finest are Wells Homestead in Riverhead and, farther east, Bayview Farm Market in Aquebogue.

Bayview is one of the largest retail farms on the East End. It's the big-box store of local farm stands, but in this case size does not detract from quality. Everything here, from the vegetables to the duck, are local and delicious, but our absolute favorites are the fruit pies. They come in either individual portions or a family size and are so tasty—crisp, flaky crust filled with tart, fresh fruit—that you might find it easy to turn a family-size pie into a single serving.

Bayview Farm Market
891 Main Road | Aquebogue, NY 11931 | (631) 722-3077

Wells Homestead

Wells Homestead is nearly impossible to overlook. The bright red barn is the centerpiece of this beautifully art-directed market. The flower and vegetable arrangements show a Fauvist sensibility—the colors explode. Bayview sells only local products, from duck eggs to milk, potato chips, and, of course, fruits and vegetables. If you feel up to it, you can also buy your seeds or small vegetable plants here and start your garden from scratch. The farm is one of the oldest in the region, having been in business nearly three hundred years.

Wells Homestead 460 Main Road | Riverhead, NY 11901 | (631) 722-3796
www.wellshomesteadmarket.com

THIS SIGN CERTIFIES THAT THE OWNER OF THIS STAND IS A BONA FIDE FARMER; AND THAT ALL PRODUCE SOLD ON THIS STAND IS LOCALLY GROWN UNLESS OTHERWISE STATED

IDAHO BAKERS .99/LB

Red "B" Potatoes 3 1.49/LB

SWEET Potato 99¢/

Hostas $10.00

Junda's Pastry Shop

Some kids are lucky and are born with a mission—and from the picture we saw of Christopher Junda, age nine, selling pies in front of his parents' house, it's clear he's one of the lucky ones. He found his calling early and still sells and bakes pastry, only now in his own shop, Junda's, in Jamesport.

You'll find Junda's in a charming eighteenth-century house, one of the finest in this architecturally blessed village. And when you enter the store, you'll feel as though you're stepping into a historic home. The pastries, sophisticated and made with great care and passion, are on display in antique cases. The log strudel, crisp and flaky, is filled with perfectly prepared fruits. Babka is another house specialty— Junda makes it from a recipe he borrowed from his Polish aunt. All the recipes are traditionally European and executed to perfection.

Junda's Pastry Shop 1612 Main Road | Jamesport, NY 11947 | (631) 722-4999

North Fork Potato Chips

Potato farming is to eastern Long Island what car making is to Detroit, and both businesses are in a similar state of decline. Rising real estate prices have driven large numbers of potato farmers off the land, dramatically reducing the number of tillable acres. To survive, the few remaining holdouts have had to find more profitable ways to market their spuds.

One delightful result of this economic pressure is North Fork Potato Chips. These world-class snacks taste the way you always imagined chips should: light and crisp and full of potato flavor. The key is simplicity. They are made with only three ingredients: potatoes grown on the Sidors' family farm, sunflower oil, and sea salt. The resulting chip is fresh, clean, and all potato. The secret is the sunflower oil, which is lighter than less-expensive vegetable oils and leaves no greasy aftertaste.

The Sidors started North Fork Potato Chips in 1993 without a bit of chip-making experience, and turned it into what it is today, a thriving family business.

North Fork Potato Chips Mattituck, NY 11952
(631) 734-2243 (warehouse) | www.northforkchips.com

Harbes Family Farms

Monica and Ed Harbes take the family part of their business very seriously—the Harbeses have eight children—and their farm stand is sure to delight every member of the family from kids to grandparents.

For the kids, depending on the season, there's a bunny farm, cow milking, pig races, and a glass-backed beehive. For all ages, there's the corn maze and U-pick pumpkins, berries, and gourds. The Harbes grow some of the best-tasting corn on Long Island, so whether you buy it by the ear to cook at home or by the bagful with their amazing popcorn, savory and sweet, be sure to try some.

Aside from a full array of vegetables, pies, and preserves, the Harbes started to cultivate grapes a few years ago, and now turn out some very good Long Island wines that the adults can sample in a white barn behind the farm stand. The Chardonnay is especially good, light and fruity, unlike many of the heavy, oaky chardonnays of California.

Harbes Family Farms
Two locations:
247 Sound Avenue | Mattituck, NY 11952 | (631) 298-0800
Main Road, Route 25 | Jamesport, NY 11947 | (631) 722-2022
www.harbesfamilyfarm.com

TY LLWYD FARM

FRESH BROWN

EGGS

FERTILE EGGS

STRAW

RED

POTATOES

CHICKEN

MANURE

Wickham's Fruit Farm

Wickham's Fruit Farm is one of the oldest and largest commercial farms on Long Island. The retail space is completely unpretentious, but if you're a pick-it-yourself fan, this is the place to stop. In June it's strawberries; in July come cherries, raspberries, blueberries, and peaches; in August, peaches, blueberries, blackberries, and raspberries; and in September, apples and more raspberries.

It's a real joy to let the kids run loose in the field. There they'll learn that berries don't grow in plastic containers and what real fruit is supposed to taste like.

Wickham's makes some of the best cinnamon and sugar donuts anywhere. Just be careful how many you buy, because it's guaranteed you will eat them all in one sitting. The preserves are also excellent, made from their own berries and put up to perfection. They spread beautifully on warm toast at breakfast time or anytime you need a taste of summer sweetness.

Wickham's Fruit Farm 28700 Main Road | Cutchogue, NY 11935 | (631) 734-5454 | www.wickhamsfruitfarm.com

STRAWBERRY TIRAMISU

Serves 6 to 8

This is an American version of Italian tiramisu. One key ingredient is fresh strawberries at the pick of the season in July, when they have the most flavor. This recipe contains raw egg, so keep all ingredients in the refrigerator until you use them, and don't keep any leftovers.

8 free-range organic eggs

1 cup sugar

1 vanilla bean

2 pounds mascarpone

1 pint fresh strawberries, hulled

1. Separate the egg yolks from the whites. Reserve the whites in the refrigerator.

2. In a mixer on high speed, combine the egg yolks with the sugar for 3 minutes. Scrape the vanilla bean and add to the mixture; discard the pod. Add the mascarpone and mix on high speed for 1 minute; reserve in the refrigerator.

3. Beat the egg whites until soft peaks form and fold into the mascarpone mixture. Reserve in the refrigerator.

4. Slice each strawberry into 4 pieces vertically. In a glass casserole about 11 x 14, layer the cheese mixture and then the strawberries. Repeat and finish with a layer of mascarpone mixture. Cover with plastic wrap and refrigerate for no more than 3 hours.

Braun Seafood

Braun Seafood in Cutchogue started out as a family-operated oyster company, plying the shellfish beds of Great Peconic Bay in classic single-sailed oyster skiffs. Today Braun's is one of the world's largest purveyors of seafood, but despite the remarkable growth, it's still a family business. And while they continue to gather and cultivate oysters in Great Peconic Bay, they also gather seafood from all over the world and bring it back to Cutchogue in their fleet of sparkling white refrigerator trucks.

Braun sits quietly next to rural Route 25, but when you drive into the parking lot you can see that it feels more like a FedEx hub than a roadside fish stall. Trucks come and go, bringing in fish from all over the world, and then redistributing it to restaurants and retail outlets all over the East End of Long Island. The retail store has the widest selection of the freshest fish you can find anywhere east of the Fulton Fish Market.

And the people behind the counter are extraordinarily helpful and knowledgeable. As you sit at one of the picnic tables outside enjoying the world-class lobster salad, you may see the eighty-year-old patriarch of the family tending the garden, pulling out weeds by hand. This is a local family business writ large, but the commitment to quality remains.

Braun Seafood 30840 Main Road | Cutchogue, NY 11935
(631) 734-5550 | www.braunseafood.com

PECONIC BAY SCALLOP STEW

Serves 4

When Ken Braun was a young boy, his father always woke him up and would make this stew for him when he got home from buying scallops in Greenport. To make it the way Ken's father did, it's important to ask your fishmonger for freshly opened Peconic Bay scallops and their natural juices. Serve with lots of crusty bread and a side salad for a hearty dinner.

½ stick butter

1 pint Peconic Bay scallops (unwashed), in their natural juices

Salt and freshly ground pepper

1 quart whole milk

1. In a saucepan, melt the butter over medium-low heat.

2. Add the scallops and their juices and season with salt and pepper to taste. Continue cooking for 4 to 5 minutes, or until the scallops are half cooked.

3. Add the milk, bring to a simmer, and simmer for 6 to 10 minutes, letting the natural scallop juices blend with the milk. Do not overheat the milk. Serve immediately.

Sang Lee Farms

This farm started in the 1940s, and though it has changed location several times as developers moved deeper up the North Fork, it is still owned by the Lee family. Fred Lee, nephew of the founder, and his wife, Karen, run the farm full-time. At one point in its history, Sang Lee Farm was the biggest wholesale producer of Asian vegetables on the East Coast, but with increased pressure from competition they have successfully branched out into retail.

The sandy North Fork soil and climate are perfect for Asian vegetables, and the farm's bok choy, mizuna, Shanghai choy, and tatsoi are excellent. You will see shapes and colors of vegetables you've never seen before, and Karen Lee, who has begun giving courses in Chinese vegetable preparation, will explain each and every one with great patience. You can also take home recipes, printed on beautifully colored card stock. Sang Lee is a great learning experience and a welcome time out from the North Fork wine trail. Don't miss the gourmet Asian sauces and salad dressing.

If you would like to support the farm and have your fresh vegetables, herbs, and fruits delivered to the city, you can participate in their Community Supported Agriculture program, or CSA. Call or visit their Web site for details.

Sang Lee Farms 25180 County Road 48 | Peconic, NY 11958
(631) 734-7001 | www.sangleefarms.com

STIR-FRIED BOK CHOY

Serves 4

Bok choy is a Chinese vegetable with a white stem and dark green leaves. It has become popular in the United States and is now widely available. If you visit Sang Lee Farms, be sure to buy their stir-fry sauce; it's one of the key ingredients.

4 to 5 tablespoons vegetable oil

1½ to 2 pounds baby bok choy, steamed, stems cut into bite-size pieces, and leaves chopped

1 carrot, julienned.

2½ ounces Sang Lee Farm's Stir-Fry Sauce

1 medium onion, chopped

1 red pepper, cored, seeded, and diced

2 scallions, diced

1. Heat 3 tablespoons of the vegetable oil in a wok or deep sauté pan over medium-high heat. When the oil is hot (a drop of water will sizzle), maintain the medium-high setting and add the bok choy stems and carrots. Toss for 1½ to 2 minutes.

2. Add the stir-fry sauce and mix to coat. Then add the onions, peppers, and bok choy leaves. Continue tossing for 1½ to 2 minutes.

3. Add the scallions and toss thoroughly for about 30 seconds. Remove from the heat and transfer to a serving platter.

Catapano Dairy Farm

As you approach Catapano Dairy Farm on North Road in Peconic, you'll be struck by the beauty of the sweeping manicured lawns. Parked on one of those lawns is a copy of Noah's Ark, which turns out to be a playground for the Catapanos' prized herd of goats.

The Catapanos' kindness and care show in the quality of the cheese they produce from the goat's milk. All of it is fresh and delicious. If you love goat cheese, this farm is a must; and if you're not sure, then Catapano's offerings will convert you. In addition to simple fresh goat cheese, light and creamy, there's also herbed goat cheese, perfect for an aperitif. The feta al fresco crumbled into a salad is perfect, the best available this side of Greece. The homemade ricotta is worlds apart from the supermarket stuff—it's light and airy, fresh like a spring day. But the absolute winner is the goat's milk yogurt. Try the vanilla—it's spectacular.

Catapano Dairy Farm 33705 North Road | Peconic, NY 11958
(631) 765-8042 | www.catapanodairyfarm.com

EGGPLANT, TOMATO, AND GOAT CHEESE SANDWICHES

Serves 6

This is one of Karen Catapano's favorites; you'll love it, too.

1½ cups chopped plum tomatoes

¼ cup chopped fresh basil

2 tablespoons red wine vinegar

Salt and pepper

1 large eggplant, sliced lengthwise into 6 pieces ½ inch thick

6 slices French bread

⅓ cup olive oil

9 ounces soft goat cheese

1. Combine the tomatoes, basil, and vinegar in a bowl. Season with salt and pepper to taste.

2. Lightly brush the 6 eggplant slices and the bread slices with the olive oil.

3. On high heat, grill the eggplant and bread slices until golden brown (about 4 minutes for the eggplant, 2 minutes for the bread).

4. Arrange the bread on a platter, spread the cheese on top of each slice, and layer an eggplant slice on top of the cheese. Season with salt and pepper.

5. Using a slotted spoon, mound the tomato mixture on top of each slice and serve.

The Farm

KK and Ira Haspel, the proprietors of the Farm, use a dowsing rod to communicate with their plants. According to KK, this is a two-way conversation. We French have a pragmatic, distinctly nonspiritual relationship with our vegetables, so I was a bit skeptical. But when I looked at these superb gardens and tasted the output, I was, if not a convert, then at least willing to learn.

This farm is biodynamic, which means that along with the interspecies communication, KK and Ira use no pesticides or fertilizers. They regulate the soil with minerals and by consulting moon cycles. They believe that healthy soil helps create stronger plants that resist invasion by pests and weeds, and they plan their planting cycles by consulting an astronomical calendar, the Stella Natura.

The proof is in the harvest. On their very small farm, KK and Ira have proved that productivity and quality can work together.

The Farm 59945 Main Road | Southold, NY 11971
(631) 765-2075 | www.kkthefarm.com

Widow's Hole Oyster Company

At the turn of the nineteenth century, large fleets of single-sail sloops plied Long Island's bays, raking the bottom for plentiful and delicious oysters. Oyster gathering became one of the area's major sources of revenue, but by 1980 the industry had disappeared, decimated by overharvesting.

Today, a new generation of independent oyster farmers has brought the business back to Peconic Bay. Among the more successful are Mike and Isabel Osinski of Greenport. The couple started Widow's Hole Oyster Company in 2004 after Mike quit his job on Wall Street. They began with just 240 oyster seeds and now grow some of the most sought-after bivalves on the East Coast.

The oysters grow undisturbed in wire baskets in the cool clear water off the Osinskis' home on Great Peconic Bay. Wednesday is delivery day, and among their customers are some of New York's finest restaurants: Le Bernardin, The Four Seasons, Oyster Bar, Bouley, and Della Femina. Widow's Hole sells several hundred thousand oysters each year, but they are careful to strike the right balance between consumption and conservation.

The best part of the visit was when Mike began shucking oysters fresh out of the bay. They were full of the clean taste of the sea that I remember as a child on Île de Ré, on France's Atlantic coast, another great place for oysters. To place an order or visit the place, leave a message on the answering machine.

Widow's Hole Oyster Company   307 Flint Street | Greenport, NY 11944 | (631) 477-3442 (phone orders) | www.widowsholeoysters.com

Aldo's

Aldo is a confident man. He runs a small coffee bar on Front Street directly across from a large Starbucks, and could not care less about the competition. What makes him so confident is the quality of his store-roasted coffee, his brilliance as a barista, and the delicious muffins and biscotti he bakes to order: They keep his customers firmly nailed to their seats.

There is no mass production here. Every cup of coffee is made with care, and regulars standing in line assure impatient newcomers that it's definitely worth the wait.

The macchiato is perfect, served in a brown ceramic cup, but don't stir it. Aldo does not approve of tampering with his creations. *Macchiato* means "stain," and Aldo will top your cup with a spot of grated chocolate if you wish. The biscotti and muffins live up to their reputation as well. They are incredibly good—and worth the wait. Aldo makes them in small batches, so they are always fresh.

Do not visit Aldo for a fast cup of coffee. Go for the experience, for the coffee, biscotti, and muffins, and for the entertaining conversation of the regulars.

Aldo's 105 Front Street │ Greenport, NY 11944 │ (631) 477-1699

Lavender by the Bay

THE NORTH FORK OF LONG ISLAND

World travelers Serge and Susan Rozenbaum bought a house in Southold and decided to give farming a try. They had seen the lavender fields in Provence and were smitten with the idea of growing the fragrant plant on the North Fork. After their first small harvest, they put a few bunches up for sale at the entrance of the property and they were gone in a flash. A new business was born.

Now the Rozenbaums own about eight acres and cultivate twenty varieties of lavender and thirty honeybee houses. From June to September, you can pick your own, but don't miss the first week of July when the acres of bright blue flowers and fragrant air are pure Provence. And if you love honey, you can have your fill at Lavender by the Bay. The flavors change during the season depending upon which flowers the bees are taking pollen from; our favorite is the lavender-infused variety.

In addition to its culinary uses, lavender is also a medicinal plant. The ancient Romans first used lavender sachets to protect and perfume their laundry, and during the winter months Susan is busy making her own versions for sale the next summer. For a good night's sleep filled with visions of South France, allow a few buds to infuse your herbal tea. Pleasant dreams indeed.

Lavender by the Bay 7540 Main Road | East Marion, NY 11939
(631) 477-1019 or (917) 251-4642 | www.lavenderbythebay.com

LAVENDER PANNA COTTA

Serves 4

Lavender has a unique flavor that complements many dishes and beverages. Try infusing it in hot water or milk. Here it is used to give a new twist to panna cotta.

---

2 teaspoons unflavored powdered gelatin

1 cup heavy cream

½ cup fresh lavender sprigs

1 cup whole milk, warmed

½ cup sugar

---

1. Soften the gelatin by dissolving it in ¼ cup of cold water.

2. In a medium saucepan, combine the cream and the lavender over medium-high heat and bring to a boil. Immediately remove from the heat.

3. Add the warm milk and the gelatin; stir for a few minutes, until the gelatin completely dissolves. Stir in the sugar until dissolved.

4. Strain the mixture through a sieve and discard the lavender.

5. Pour into 4 small ramekins and allow to set in the refrigerator for at least 3 hours. To unmold, immerse the bottom of the ramekins in hot water and invert onto a plate.

Mark It with G

The macaroon is no ordinary biscuit. Macaroon aficionados are as passionate about these little cakes as truffle hounds are about fungus, and they hold makers to an exacting standard. In France the "Three Dieties of the Macaroon" are Pierre Hermé, Dalloyau, and Ladurée. Every Parisian has a favorite among the three, and a score of reasons why their choice is the best. Soft or hard crust, the consistency of the filling, and, of course, the flavors, to name a few. Pierre Hermé rocked the world when he came out with a truffle-flavored macaroon. In a rare occurrence, Paris was shocked.

Reed and Jesse Boone traveled to Paris, tried them all, and decided to return to Shelter Island and make the best macaroons this side of Pierre Hermé. They've succeeded. The couple first opened a tiny store on Route 114 and, after selling out of their macaroons, croissants, and quiche every day, decided to expand. They enlarged the bakery and added a restaurant, all in a charming Shelter Island farmhouse.

Reed talks about her macaroon breakthrough as a Eureka moment, and it truly was. Mark It with G macaroons come in four different flavors—chocolate, raspberry, butter cream, coffee, and pistachio—all presented in a gorgeous box. But then, a great macaroon deserves nothing less.

Mark It with G 27 N. Ferry Road | Shelter Island, NY 11964
(631) 749-5293 | www.markitwithg.com

The Wineries of Long Island

Thirty-five years ago, Alex and Louisa Hargrave decided to start a vineyard on a potato farm in Mattituck. Long Island had no history of winemaking, and the flat, sandy fields hardly conjure visions of Burgundy or Napa Valley. The initial reaction to their venture was: Potatoes, yes. Viniculture, huh?

But the Hargraves were smart, hard-working, and passionate about their idea: They wanted to bring viniferous grapes, those that make pinot noir and cabernet, to the East Coast, where they'd never been grown before. Their timing was superb, for land was still relatively cheap on the North Fork and a lot of the old farming families were happy to sell.

Many of us have romantic ideas about winemaking, but it's an extremely tough business, with all the exigencies of farming and all the uncertainty and risk of marketing a new product to a discerning audience. In the beginning, the prospect of quality wines from Long Island was met with indifference. There were booming wine industries in California, France, Italy, Spain, Argentina, Chile, and Australia, and a tiny producer on the North Fork registered on no one's radar.

But the Hargraves held strong. By combining Louisa's determination in the field and Alex's tenacity at marketing, the couple slowly built a reputation for excellent wine. People began to notice. Less alcoholic and forward than their California counterparts, the early Long Island wines were closer in style to the more subtle European types while retaining a uniquely local character. Soon other brave pioneers followed. Now the stretch along Route 25 from Aquebogue to Greenport is a wonderful

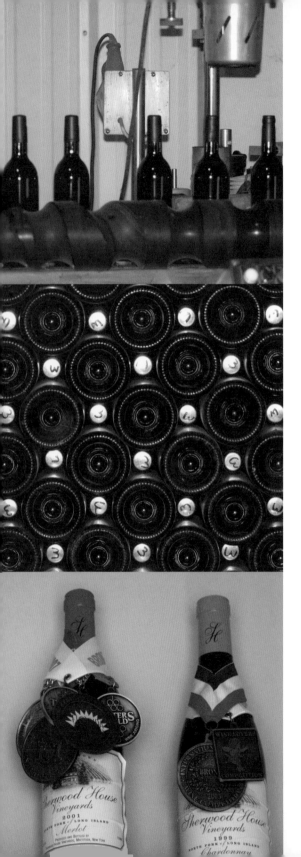

wine trail full of exciting wineries and surprisingly good wines. The movement has since jumped Peconic Bay and spread to the South Fork as well.

So, from one young couple's fantasy of owning a winery an entire industry has grown. Long Island wine is legitimate: high in quality and able to compete on a world stage. As a result, New York has become the third largest wine-growing region in America. Long Island leads the state in production, producing more than 500,000 cases annually. The number of acres under cultivation has risen from just seventeen in 1973 to around four thousand today, and for the past decade the number of visitors to East End wineries has reached well over a million.

TRAVELING THE TRAIL

The Long Island Wine Trail extends along Route 25 on the North Fork, with a couple excellent outliers on the South Fork. The vineyards run the gamut, from commercial tasting halls with tour buses stacked out front to tiny artisanal makers who bottle only enough wine to supply a shortlist of subscribers.

We concentrated on the artisanal makers, and of those there are more than enough to make for a memorable wine weekend. (By the way, if you're planning this sort of trip, you'll need a designated driver. And it is imperative to learn the old wine-tasters' trick of spitting into a bucket; otherwise what could have been a sensational treat for the discerning palate can quickly turn into a colossal hangover.) Here were our choices, but feel free to be spontaneous and try any on the list on pages 268–70.

Heading east on the North Fork's Route 25, the first stop is Paumanok Vineyards. Run by Ursula and Charles Massoud, this lovely farm produces some of the best cabernet sauvignons and Bordeaux-type blends on the island; the chenin blanc is excellent, too. The quality here is consistently first rate. And it's a great place for a picnic.

Next up is Comtesse Thérèse. This, too, is a family-managed vineyard, and you'll even find Thérèse's parents among the vines. This is the only local vineyard to use Russian and Hungarian oak barrels, and the resulting Russian Oak Chardonnay and Hungarian Oak Merlot are extraordinary.

A bit down the road is Macari Vineyards, run by two generations of the Macari family. They are dedicated to a more natural and sustainable approach to winemaking, using the principles of biodynamic farming, which emphasize soil care and composting. Their merlots, syrahs, and sauvignon blancs are excellent.

Continuing on, you'll come to Bedell Cellars, which was founded by Kip Bedell. A few years ago he sold the vineyard to film producer Michael Lynne, who has put together a talented and versatile winemaking team that includes Bedell, Pascal Marty (formerly of Mouton Rothschild), and winemaker Kelly Urbanik. They've also refurbished the facilities; the gardens are especially beautiful and definitely worth a stop.

Next is Lenz Winery, one of the most respected vineyards on Long Island. It was there that we were given a crash course in winemaking by Lenz's winemaker-in-residence, Eric Fry. With his graying ponytail and flowered shirts, Fry looks as though he could be a roadie for the Grateful Dead. But his knowledge of winemaking is so deep, and his passion for his wines so great, that it quickly becomes apparent he is the star of the show.

The first thing we learned was why the vinifera wines do so well on the flat fields of the North Fork, when in Europe and California the

ideal growing spot is the sunny side of a hill. Fry's answer: drainage. Grapes hate wet soil. So the faster the water drains, the better it is for the grapes. In Europe and California, the rich loamy soil needs a helping hand from gravity: water slides down the hill, leaving the roots high and dry, and the vines flourish. On Long Island, the sandy glacial soil acts like a water vacuum. Ten minutes after a heavy rain, the topsoil is dry. So it turns out that the same feature that made these fields great for potatoes also makes them ideal for grapes.

Next, Fry took us through a rigorous routine of tasting. We sampled new wine, still fizzy, right from the vat. Frankly, until we got to the good stuff, we were a little lost. (Fry kept pressing us for adjectives, and I kept saying, "sour apples.") But it is definitely an education and worth the time. Then came the aged wines—the merlots, cabernets, and chardonnays—and they are truly remarkable. With much less alcohol than California or Australian wines, these really had a European air, though each was uniquely Lenz. The 2001 Old Vines Merlot, which is produced in such small quantities that it is available only by subscription, was sumptuous and subtle, with strong notes of raspberry. Fry follows the traditional méthode Champenoise to produce a delightfully tart, fruity, and refreshing sparkling wine. He spent hours talking to us about his wines, and we could tell he'd barely warmed up, but we were getting a little tipsy and it was time to move on. Do not miss Lenz Vineyards.

Other noteworthy vineyards along the way are Pellegrini—who make a great merlot and whose ice wine is a perfect accompaniment to dessert—as well as Diliberto Winery, on Peconic Bay, and Shinn Estate, which is one of the prettiest spots we visited.

On the South Fork, where real estate costs are about double those on the North Fork, two standouts beckon. The first is Channing Daughters. With a cutting-edge philosophy and the belief that Long Island is white wine country, the team at this estate is constantly experimenting with varieties and blends. The second is Wölffer Estates, a beautiful vineyard attached to an elegant riding facility. The tasting room is Tuscan by way of Napa Valley, and the highlight here is the rosé, which easily competes with the pink stuff from the south of France.

The Hudson Valley and the Catskills

Officially, the Hudson River Valley begins in upper West-chester County and extends northward past Bear Mountain, Storm King, and West Point to Troy, just north of Albany. But for me, the Hudson Valley begins just above the George Washington Bridge in New York City, at the Palisades. For a Parisian who grew up beside the walled-in hypercivilized Seine, those raw stone cliffs across the river from the packed streets of upper Manhattan echo the pure and delightful dissonance between urban nuttiness on the one bank, and natural grandeur on the other.

However you define its boundaries, the Hudson Valley is a magnificent stretch of cliff, mountain, rolling country-side, pasture, and some of the richest farmland anywhere on the East Coast. The land has historically been used for dairy farming, animal husbandry, and a bit of truck farming. In 2005 New York State was the third largest milk producer in the country, behind California and Wisconsin.

But the Hudson Valley's proximity to New York City made it attractive as a locale for second homes, and more and more of the Hudson Valley's dairy and vegetable farms were converted to equestrian facilities and hunting preserves. This saves the land from the developer's bulldozer, but it doesn't do much to forward the cause of local food production.

But over the past fifteen years, there has been a rejuvenating new synergy. The nearby Culinary Institute of America has grown rapidly, turning out scores of professional foodies already familiar with the region. Farmers' markets have boomed, with increased demand especially from New York City Greenmarkets. And then there is the burgeoning locavore movement and the growth of CSAs (see page 16). Conventional farmers have realized that organic and biodynamic farming methods, aside from being better for people, can be more profitable and create new markets for their products. This perfect convergence of events—led by the spirit, energy, determination, and wisdom of some remarkable agriventurers—has transformed the Hudson Valley and parts of the adjacent Catskill region into a thriving hub of new-age agriculture.

THE HUDSON VALLEY

The Kneaded Bread

Sometimes you find great food where you least expect it. Main Street in Port Chester, New York, looks a little rundown, but when you walk into this corner bakery you will be transported by the beautiful display of bread and the heady smells of baking wafting from the ovens. A large marble island at the center of the store is piled high with aged provolone loaf, calamata olive loaf, ciabatta, French baguette, potato rosemary loaf, raisin walnut bread, Irish soda bread, scones, cookies (oatmeal, ginger), muffins, cupcakes, focaccia, and pies.

On one side of the store is a marble coffee bar and tables, and on the other is a large refrigerator full of fresh products and sandwiches. Joe Bastianich, a chef at one of the Mario Batali restaurants in Port Chester, raves about Kneaded Bread's tuna sandwich.

As soon as you meet Jennifer Kohn, the energetic proprietor, and her husband, Jeffrey, you understand that the attraction of the place runs deeper than the great breads and coffee. She pays close attention to every customer, to the quality of her bread, making sure there are no empty spaces. The two have been working together for some time now.

At the Kneaded Bread, everything is done by hand. Bakers start working by midnight to make sure there is fresh bread on the shelves by the time they open in the morning. They use only unbleached, unbromated flour and natural ingredients.

The Kneaded Bread 181 North Main Street | Port Chester, NY 10573
(914) 937-9489 | www.kneadedbread.com

GAZPACHO

Every morning around ten at the Kneaded Bread, the gazpacho is presented in a huge copper pot and put on display. People are there waiting for it, and by lunchtime it's sold out. This recipe is one of their most popular appetizers, especially when served with slices of their seven-grain bread. In the summer, made with fresh vegetables and croutons, it becomes a meal in itself. Serve with the bread.

4 seedless cucumbers, peeled

¼ jalapeño pepper, seeded and roughly chopped

½ red onion, roughly chopped

1 garlic clove, peeled

1 red bell pepper, seeded and roughly chopped

⅓ cup chopped Italian parsley

½ cup Spanish sherry vinegar

1 large can Sacramento tomato juice

½ cup olive oil

¼ cup extra virgin olive oil

Salt and pepper

Tabasco sauce

1. In the bowl of a food processor, combine the cucumbers, jalapeño, red onion, garlic, bell pepper, and parsley and pulse until chopped. While processing, add the vinegar. Add half the can of tomato juice and puree. Continue processing and add the remainder of the tomato juice and olive oils to create an emulsion. Season with salt, pepper, and Tabasco sauce to taste.

2. Chill in the refrigerator for a few hours before serving.

Stone Barns Center for Food & Agriculture

In the early 1800s, Washington Irving set many of his tales among the undulating hills, pastures, and woodlands of Sleepy Hollow, a once tiny village overlooking the Hudson River at Tappan Zee. At the beginning of the twentieth century, John D. Rockefeller decided to build his family estate, Kykuit, in this magnificent countryside. The Rockefeller family estate at one time occupied more than four thousand acres in Pocantico Hills. Some of the land is still private, but over the years the family has given large tracts to New York State for public use. Rockefeller State Park stretches over a thousand or so acres, criss-crossed with deep woods and riding trails.

The most recent gift, granted in 2004 by David Rockefeller in memory of his wife, Peggy, is the eighty-acre Stone Barns Center for Food & Agriculture. The mission of this nonprofit organization is to "celebrate, teach, and advance community-based food production and enjoyment, from farm to classroom to plate." Stone Barns lives up to its mantra. Centered on the beautiful structures—built in the 1930s by John D. Rockefeller Jr.—and radiating out into the woods and fields that surround them, it is a truly self-contained community farm, market, and kitchen.

As you walk through the fields, you are struck by the brilliant organization of the place. In one field the sheep, guarded by a white dog, lay in the shade of an old tree. In another the chickens lay eggs in their mobile coops— they look a little like the circus wagons in *Dumbo*—an arrangement that lets them move to fresh pasture so they can graze on new grass and insects every day. The resulting eggs have deep orange yolks, full of protein and essential omega-3s.

The vegetable gardens cover several acres of rolling hillside, and the well-tended plants grow according to the seasons. All the cultivation is organic: no pesticides, enriched with compost made on the farm and natural fertilizers. The compost operation is enormous and, like everything else at Stone Barns, is precisely organized. The beehives flourish between the flower fields and the sheep and produce gallons of honey along with essential pollination.

In a valley behind the barns, white greenhouses cover several acres. This is where the seedlings grow to maturity and vegetables (arugula, spinach, and kale) thrive throughout the winter. The roofs are motorized and computer controlled; they open and close to maintain a constant

Stone Barns Center for Food & Agriculture 630 Bedford Road | Pocantico Hills, NY 10591 | (914) 366-6200
www.stonebarnscenter.org

temperature inside. Geese wander freely through the fields. In one barn we saw heritage turkey, ready to be released into the woods; in another, mature Berkshire hogs. But the real treat was in the woods, where the Berkshire sows live in the open with their offspring: deep in the shady forest we saw a big sow feeding eight very hungry piglets.

The purpose of this farm is not just to produce locally appropriate, sustainably grown food, which it does magnificently, but to show visitors the importance of this kind of farming and to teach students how to do it themselves. Many of the farmworkers are apprentices and student interns learning agricultural methods on the job.

Much of the food grown at Stone Barns goes to local farmers' markets and supplies the excellent Blue Hill Café and the beautiful world-class Blue Hill at Stone Barns restaurant, located in one of the barn buildings. Although the restaurant operates independently, the chefs work closely with the farmers and try to fashion as much of the menu as possible from food grown on the farm. Set aside an afternoon and enjoy the beauty and bounty of the remarkable gift Stone Barns offers to the community.

Table Local Market

Table Local Market in Bedford Hills is a beautifully designed indoor venue dedicated to making local and sustainably grown food. Their mission begins with the store itself, built with salvaged wood and recycled materials, with sayings about food stenciled on the barn-board walls: "Eating is an agricultural act: Wendell Berry." The result is a warm and welcoming space. You'll feel like spending the whole morning there, and you'll likely run into several customers who visit every day for lunch.

Table opened in 2009, and almost since the first day the buzz has been positive. There was a market at the same location for the previous twenty years, so the former owner and the community were happy to see the tradition continue. Table's owners promote local farmers, organic businesses, and a few biodynamic farms, with most of the produce coming from New York and Connecticut. Among those represented are Mountain Product Smoke House, Amawalk Farm, Madura Farm, Mecox Dairy, Sprout Creek Farm, and John Boy's Mountain Farm.

Chef Jonathan Pratt makes all the delicious prepared food. You can sit at one of the handmade stone tables right in the store and try a few of his excellent creations. Customers all seem to want to say something supportive about Table and its owners: "The tomato tart is amazing…

great to have a place like this in Bedford Hills…try to understand what a unique place this is."

Here's some of what you'll find as you explore the aisles: red quinoa, organic peanut butter, almond butter, almonds, and pecans. In the prepared food section, everything is presented inside a beautiful terra-cotta jar. The meat section is quite complete and the butchers are knowledgeable and ready to give good advice. And you can enjoy with a clear conscience as everything is designed with an eye to recycling, conservation, and responsible living: The plates are made from corn and cutlery from potato starch; all are completely biodegradable.

This is a don't-miss stop if you're in northern Westchester County.

Table Local Market 11 Babbitt Road | Bedford Hills, NY 10507 | (914) 241-0269 | www.tablelocalmarket.com

CRÊPES WITH CORN AND MUSHROOMS

Makes 6 crêpes

This is a true locavore recipe: almost all the ingredients can come from the Hudson Valley and can be found at Table. But if you can't make the trip there, local products from your neighborhood farm stand will do. Just remember to season lightly—the taste of the farm-fresh corn should pop in your mouth.

FOR THE CRÊPES

2 eggs

1 cup nonhomogenized whole milk

½ cup whole wheat flour

3 tablespoons cultured, salted farm butter, melted

½ cup all-purpose flour, plus more as needed

FOR THE MUSHROOM FILLING AND CORN SAUCE

1 shallot or ½ red onion, minced

Kernels from 6 ears of corn

3 to 4 tablespoons butter or olive oil, plus more for the pan

½ teaspoon minced fresh thyme

1 cup chopped assorted wild mushrooms

Salt and pepper

1 cup heavy cream

1. In a bowl, mix together eggs, milk, whole wheat flour, and 2 tablespoons of the butter. Add the all-purpose flour, a tablespoon at a time, to create the consistency of thick heavy cream. Let the batter rest for 10 minutes.

2. Heat a sauté pan with the remaining tablespoon of butter; wipe out the excess. Pour just enough batter to coat the bottom of the pan, constantly rotating the pan to form a circle. Cook the crêpe just until the edges begin to pull away. Flip and cook the other side for another 20 seconds. Stack the crêpes and tent with foil to keep warm until you're ready to assemble.

3. Create the filling: In a medium saucepan, sauté the shallot in the butter or oil until translucent. Add the corn (and more butter if the pan is dry), stir to coat, and cook until soft, 3 to 5 minutes. Season with salt and pepper to taste. Remove from the heat. Reserve half the corn and set aside. To the remaining mixture in the saucepan, add the mushrooms and cook for 2 minutes, until the mushrooms are soft. Add the thyme, stir for 1 minute, and season with salt and pepper to taste. Set aside.

4. Prepare the sauce: Place the reserved corn mixture in a blender and puree while pouring in the heavy cream in a slow stream. Warm the mixture in a small saucepan before assembling the crêpes.

5. Assemble the crêpes: Spoon 2 to 3 tablespoons of the mushroom filling into each crêpe, fold or roll the crêpe (whichever you prefer), and garnish with a tablespoon of the corn sauce.

Heinchon's Ice Cream Parlor

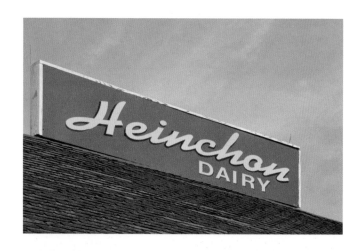

Heinchon's Ice Cream Parlor is one of those places that proves you don't need great decor to get great food. Inside a scantily marked rundown yellow house in the middle of a dirt parking lot is some of the best ice cream you'll ever have.

Everything is made with the freshest milk from Heinchon Dairy, and the flavors are extreme in the extreme. The black raspberry is intense, like putting your face into an ice-cold black raspberry pie. The Hudson Valley Harvest Vanilla is pure powerful vanilla. The raspberry swirl and ginger flavor also pack a wallop. For a lighter treat, the frozen yogurt is excellent; the pumpkin flavor was our favorite. And the toppings are as concentrated: homemade hot fudge, butterscotch, and whipped cream. All the flavors are 100 percent natural.

Heinchon's Ice Cream Parlor
Route 22 | Pawling, NY 12564 | (845) 878-6262

Sprout Creek Farm

If you've ever had the urge to toss it all in and trade your SUV for a tractor, Sprout Creek Farm is a great place to test the depth of your conviction.

Sprout Creek is a two-hundred-acre educational farm dedicated to teaching the art of farming to children and adults as a way to instill a sense of community, responsibility, and social conscience. Amid a setting of natural beauty and intellectual inquiry, you and your family can learn to milk cows, make cheese, care for animals, and savor the peaceful rhythms and responsibilities of farm life.

The farm was founded by the Society of the Sacred Heart in 1982, and today more than five thousand students a year participate in the summer and year-long educational programs. Sprout Creek is often booked well in advance by school groups, so plan accordingly, but it offers a great way to get a taste of farm life and appreciate the hard work and discipline that go into bringing food to the table. Don't miss their excellent cheeses.

Sprout Creek Farm 34 Lauer Road | Poughkeepsie, NY 12603
(845) 485-9885 | www.sproutcreekfarm.org

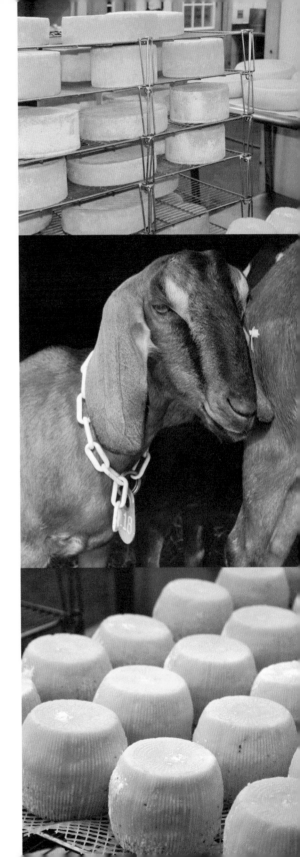

Fishkill Farms

After Josh Morgenthau graduated from Yale, he thought momentarily about the traditional family businesses, banking and politics, and decided instead to give farming a try. He did have a bit of a head start: a family farm in Fishkill, New York, bought by his grandfather Henry before becoming Franklin D. Roosevelt's Secretary of the Treasury.

Josh converted the gentleman's orchard into a working farm, adding chickens, vegetables, and a store to row upon row of fruit trees: cherry, peach, nectarine, and apple. The store carries everything grown on the farm, plus foods such as cheeses, milk, and grass-fed beef from local producers. On display is a great collection of political mementos, including photographs of FDR's visit to the farm.

And don't miss the egg mobile. The eggs here are terrific.

Fishkill Farms 9 Fishkill Farm Road | Hopewell Junction, NY 12533
(845) 897-4377 | www.fishkillfarms.com

Uncle Neilie's Maple Syrup

Sometimes people find their avocation by sheer chance. When Neil Kane moved to Rhinebeck many years ago, he admired the huge sugar maples on his property but didn't think much past that. Somewhere along the way he read about maple syrup production in Vermont, and eventually he started tapping a few of his own trees.

From those few buckets of sap processed in an outdoor evaporator, Uncle Neilie's Maple Syrup was born. Neil continued to grow his small start-up until today he produces sixty-four gallons a year in his beautiful sugaring barn. When not tapping trees, evaporating sap, or bottling syrup, Neil is out looking for wood to fuel the evaporator. He believes the wood gives his syrup its remarkable taste.

The process is arduous. Until it is distilled, the sap is delicate and spoils easily, so Neil has devised an underground storage system that keeps it at the right temperature. After the sap is evaporated to exactly the right consistency, the syrup is filtered and then stored in sterilized pots.

If you visit the farm in February and March, you will be welcomed to watch, learn, and even help as Neil makes his delicious syrup. You can buy it at a stand in front of the farm or from Gigi Hudson Valley Market, farther up Route 9 in nearby Red Hook (see page 232).

Uncle Neilie's Maple Syrup 38 Mill Road | Rhinebeck, NY 12572
(845) 876-3894 | neilbev81@hotmail.com

Wild Hive Farm Store

Wild Hive on Main Street in beautiful Clinton Corners is one of the best and most distinctive bakeries we've come upon. What makes it unique is that all their products contain flours made with grain they mill themselves, and they bake everything in a wood-burning oven. This is a truly self-contained, local bakery, based on the old European miller/baker model. Don Lewis, the baker/miller and owner, controls the whole process, from buying the grain to milling it to baking, packaging, and selling.

Don is dedicated to the idea of sustainable, local food and buys all his grain from nearby farmers; he then mills the grain in a stone mill he bought several years ago. Wild Hive uses the flour to make bread, but they also sell it by the pound. These artisanal flours will change the taste of any flour-based dish for the better, and, because it's hand-milled, the flour is richer in nutrients, too.

We recommend the triticale, which is a hybrid of wheat and rye and especially rich in protein—great for making pasta and granola. You can also try stone-ground rye, polenta, and spelt. We tried the polenta, and it was the richest, creamiest, most flavorful we've ever had.

Every morning Don bakes small batches of bread in his wood-burning oven. The day we were there he had walnut raisin, rosemary garlic, Irish soda bread, and whole-grain spelt. We took home a loaf of the spelt bread, dense and rich. Toasted with a little goat cheese, it makes a full meal.

Don started out as a beekeeper and slowly found his way to his true calling, and we are very happy he did. If you visit Clinton Corners, plan to have lunch at the Wild Hive Café. The quiche and vegetable pies are excellent.

Wild Hive Farm Store 2411 Salt Point Turnpike | Clinton Corners, NY 12514 | (845) 266-5863 | www.wildhivefarm.com

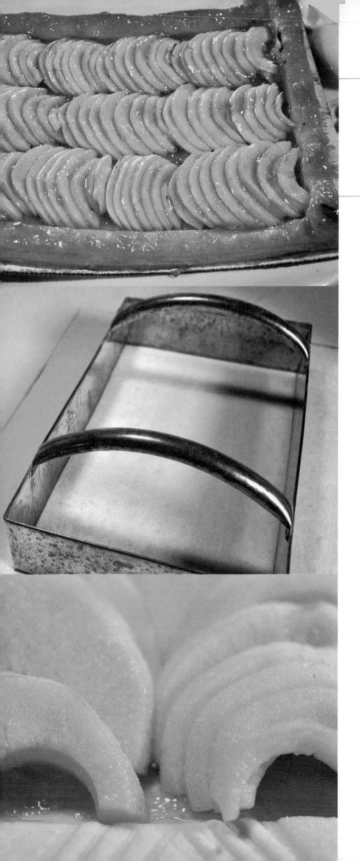

The Art of the Tart

About five years ago Kate Weiner moved out of the city to Clinton Corners. She wanted a "human-sized" life and a chance to be closer to her husband. We visited Kate to learn about her tarts, but we also received a lesson in how to live an exemplary life, doing exactly what you've always dreamed of doing.

Kate told us, "There is more to this than the tart. I love my customers. I meet remarkable people—people who care about food. So, I want to make one thing really well, and I think I have succeeded. I dream about having the perfect equipment. I think about interesting combinations of fruits and flavors: apricot with saffron was the first one for my glaze." Her two inspirations are Julia Child and Madame Dumas, the brilliant patissière.

Kate is a true craftsman, and she spends the entire workweek building tarts for sale at the Saturday Market in Millbrook. Every morning at ten her husband gives her a kiss and leaves for work, and Kate heads to the kitchen to do her own work. A typical week goes like this:

On Monday she assembles all the boxes and stamps each one with her logo. She also makes the dough in small batches, using only high-fat-content European butter between the exquisitely thin pastry sheets. Then she puts the dough aside to settle.

On Tuesday she prepares the glaze. The recipe is a secret, but we can tell you that it takes a lot of work.

Tuesday is also laundry day; tablecloths and clothes for the market have to be sparkling.

On Wednesday she shops for the freshest ingredients and looks for inspiration in the available fruits and vegetables. When we arrived she was about to set some very ripe and pungent tomatoes to roast slowly for the next ten hours.

On Thursday she rolls out the dough and shapes the tarts. For a recent birthday Kate's husband gave her a rectangular dough cutter, and that shape has become her signature. She also sautés the onions for her wonderful pissaladière tart.

On Friday she prepares the fruits and vegetables, depending upon the season. She may poach pears in brandy or precisely slice apples to be soaked in lemon juice.

Now for the truly obsessive part. Kate wakes up every Saturday morning at two to bake. Clearly she could do this the day before, but for ultimate freshness she wants her tarts coming out of the oven only a few hours before they're sold at the market. She bakes about sixty tarts in her small noncommercial convection oven, and then around six her husband comes down, makes coffee, helps her box them up, loads the car, and drives her to the market, where her tarts sell out within a couple hours.

The Art of the Tart 153 Knight Road | Clinton Corners, NY 12514 | (845) 868-7107 | Theartofthetart@gmail.com

The Currant Company

Although black currants are enormously popular in Europe and Canada, they were banned for growth in the United States from the late 1800s. The plants carried a disease called white blister pine rust that threatened to kill off America's pine forests. Before the ban, Native Americans had long used currants medicinally; the intensely flavored berries are rich in vitamins and antioxidants, more so than blueberries or pomegranates.

Canadians, also big currant fans, have developed disease-resistant hybrids, and thanks to Greg Quinn, who owns the Currant Company in Clinton Corners, cassis is back in the USA.

Attracted by the fruit's beneficial qualities as well as its wonderful flavor, Greg—a former TV actor, linguist, restaurant owner, and botany teacher—put his eclectic skills to work and successfully lobbied for the currant's return to favor. The ban was reversed, and now Greg grows red and black varieties on his beautiful Catskill farm.

You can buy currant bushes from the farm to plant yourself, or you can order frozen fruits from their Web site. Either way it's great to see that a distinguished, timeless, and healthy flavor note has found its way back into the American culinary vocabulary.

The Currant Company 59 Walnut Lane | Staatsburg, NY 12580
(845) 266-8299 | www.currantc.com

CURRANTC SORBET

Serves 8

Greg Quinn, owner of the Currant Company and previously a chef in Europe, has many recipes. In fact, one of his passions is to collect as many as possible. If you would like to prepare an entire meal with currants, his Web site is filled with recipes to try. To make this one you'll need crème de cassis, found at your local wine store.

¼ cup sugar

2 tablespoons light corn syrup

3 cups CurrantC Premium Black Currant Nectar

¼ cup crème de cassis

---

1. In a medium pot, bring the sugar, corn syrup, and ½ cup of the black currant nectar to a boil, stirring until the sugar is dissolved. Boil for 1 minute more. Transfer to a metal bowl and stir in the crème de cassis and the remaining 2½ cups black currant nectar.

2. Set the bowl within a larger bowl filled with ice and cold water and let the mixture stand, stirring occasionally, until cold, about 10 minutes.

3. Freeze in an ice cream maker according to the manufacturer's instructions; then transfer to an airtight container and place in the freezer to harden for at least 1 hour.

MINESTRONE ALLA GENOVESE

Serves 6

This recipe came to us from the beloved chef Pino Luongo, who has run many restaurant kitchens in Manhattan. Minestrone is traditionally made with pasta or rice, but Chef Luongo's twist on this old Italian favorite features corn and pesto. This recipe is really more a template; feel free to substitute your own favorite combination of vegetables based on what's at the farmers' market. Fresh cranberry beans are in season in the late summer and early fall; the rest of the year you can use dried beans instead. But in that case be sure to soak them first in water for 8 hours or overnight, drain, and rinse thoroughly.

1 cup fresh cranberry beans

1 cup fresh green beans, cut into small pieces

2 medium potatoes, cut into small cubes

2 large zucchini, cut into small cubes

1 cup fresh or frozen English peas

1 cup fresh or frozen corn

¼ cup extra virgin olive oil

Salt and pepper

½ cup prepared pesto

6 tablespoons grated Parmigiano-Reggiano cheese

1. In a large pot, bring 3 quarts of water to a boil over medium-high heat. Add both types of beans and the potatoes, reduce the heat, and simmer for 10 minutes; then add the zucchini, English peas, and corn.

2. Continue to simmer over medium heat for an additional 20 minutes, and then add the olive oil and salt and pepper to taste. If the vegetables or beans are still a bit crunchy, cook the soup a little longer, until they are tender and almost falling apart. If you need more liquid, add water to create a soupy consistency.

3. Remove from the heat and let the soup rest for 15 minutes. To serve, place a heaping tablespoon of pesto in each soup plate, mix in a tablespoon of cheese, and ladle the soup over the top. Serve immediately.

Migliorelli Farm

In 1933 Angelo Migliorelli emigrated to America from the Lazio region of Italy with only a change of clothes and a sack of rapini seeds. (Rapini is better known as broccoli rabe.) Three quarters of a century later, the Migliorellis have parlayed their grandfather's passion for these pungent greens into a thriving produce business, with three stores and more than six hundred acres of Hudson Valley farmland under cultivation.

To farm those acres Ken Migliorelli, Angelo's grandson, uses the European Good Agriculture Practice, a system that greatly reduces the need for dangerous pesticides. In 1998 he agreed to a conservation easement, which means that his land will be farmland forever.

All fruits and vegetables picked on the Migliorelli farm are sold within twenty-four hours, so if you buy from one of their stores, you can be sure about freshness. Ken's partner Mercedes Wallner recently opened a charming fruit and vegetable store in Hudson, New York, and added local cheeses and baked goods to the mix. Now you can combine a day of antique hunting along Main Street with some serious food shopping.

Migliorelli Farm
46 Freeborn Lane | Tivoli, NY 12583 | (845) 757-3276 | www.migliorelli.com

Migliorelli Farm Stand
668 River Road | Rhinebeck, NY 12572

Migliorelli Farm Store
302 Warren Street | Hudson, NY 12534 | (518) 828-3277

Quattro's Game Farm

At first glance Quattro's looks like a wild-game version of a pick-your-own lobster shop. On one side of the store are dressed birds and venison steaks displayed under glass, and on the other is an armory—racks of shotguns and rifles. All are for sale. But although you can buy a gun at Quattro's, you can't shoot a bird or a deer there.

But what you can do is locate just about every edible bird imaginable, including pheasant, four species of turkey, geese, and ducks, with many heritage breeds. They also sell venison when in season. This is a great place to get your Thanksgiving turkey, but be sure to order well in advance. In the spring, you can buy fresh eggs, duck, chicken, and pheasant, each with its own distinctive taste.

Quattro's Game Farm
Route 44 | Pleasant Valley, NY 12569 | (845) 635-2018

BAKED BREADED CHICKEN BREASTS

Serves 4

This comes from one of our favorite restaurants in New York City, Da Silvano. Sometimes the simplest dishes are the most satisfying. Once in a while, there's nothing better than breaded chicken breasts pan-fried in a combination of butter and olive oil and then baked in the oven. A squeeze of fresh lemon lightens the flavor of the fried breadcrumbs. Serve with spinach sautéed in olive oil and garlic.

1 cup dried breadcrumbs

4 boneless chicken breast halves from two 1-pound breasts

2 tablespoons olive oil

2 tablespoons unsalted butter

Fine sea salt

Freshly ground pepper

1 lemon, cut into 4 wedges

1. Preheat the oven to 350 degrees F.

2. Spread the breadcrumbs onto a clean, dry surface and roll the chicken pieces in them, pressing down lightly to make sure they adhere to the meat.

3. In an ovenproof sauté pan large enough to hold all 4 breasts, warm the olive oil and melt the butter over medium heat. Add the breaded chicken and cook for 2 minutes on each side. As the chicken cooks, season each side with salt and pepper to taste.

4. Transfer the pan to the oven and bake until the chicken is cooked through, 7 to 10 minutes. Cut one breast open with a knife to check for doneness.

5. Remove the pan from the oven and transfer the chicken to a serving platter. Serve the lemon wedges alongside.

Coach Farm

Coach Farm is to goat cheese what West Virginia is to coal mining; they own the category. Miles and Lillian Cahn started the farm from scratch after selling their first business, the Coach Leatherwear company. What began as an escapist fantasy with a few scraggly billy goats has turned into a thriving farm, home to more than a thousand French Alpine purebred goats. It produces some of the best goat cheeses you'll find anywhere in the world.

The farm is self-contained, a micro-ecosystem outside Gallatinville, New York. Coach grows all the hay and grain used to feed their goats, and they control every step of the milking, cheese making, and packaging. Everything happens on the farm. The goats are milked twice a day, and their milk goes directly from the creamery to the fromagerie. Each goat produces about a gallon of milk a day, and it takes about ten gallons to make a pound of cheese. In the ultraclean cheese-making facility, experienced workers hand-ladle curds from the milk. This is a delicate process that allows the curd to retain much of its original flavor and texture. It's one of the traits that sets artisanal goat cheese apart from the mass-produced varieties.

There are no caves here to age the cheese, but rather a series of temperature-controlled rooms. The cheese is aged for thirty to sixty-nine days, depending on the type; the stronger the flavor, the longer the aging process. The triple cheese is especially delicious, and the tart goat milk is a nice change of pace. Try it the next time a recipe calls for plain milk; it really makes a difference. Coach makes a delicious goat-milk yogurt they call Yo-Goat. It is low in sugar and carbohydrates, and kids love the taste and the packaging.

Coach Farm 105 Mill Hill Road | Pine Plains, NY 12567 | (518) 398-5325
www.coachfarm.com

Beth's Farm Kitchen

Beth's Farm Kitchen offers some of the best jams, preserves, and chutneys you'll find anywhere. And when you see all the hard work, care, creativity, and expertise that Beth and her team put into making them, you will easily understand why this is so. The work is intense. Beth, her partner Liz, and ten other women toil in a steaming kitchen, making the jam one batch at a time.

The first step is canvassing local farms for the freshest fruits and vegetables available. Beth always buys whatever's at its peak whenever she finds it. Even if she can't make the jam right away, she can peel and cut the fruit and freeze it for later use. The women make their preserves from more than thirty-nine different fruits and vegetables and buy only from local farmers. The flavors run from standards like strawberry, cranberry, and black currant to exotics including ramp, fern, and elderberry.

Next comes pureeing the fruits and vegetables. For this, Beth and her team use a gigantic food processor that looks more like a jackhammer than a Cuisinart. It takes two to three people, and a lot of muscle, to operate the oversize machine. For the cooking, here too Beth takes a different approach. Because she uses only fruits and vegetables at the peak of ripeness, she adds about a third less sugar than is used in traditional jams. She cooks only small batches to control the flavor and color.

Then there are the blends. In Beth's thirty years of jam making, she's tried just about every combination. The most popular is strawberry-rhubarb, and among the wilder combos are garlic-rosemary and hot plum chutney. You can't buy the preserves at the store, but you can order them online.

Beth's Farm Kitchen P.O. Box 113 | Stuyvesant Falls, NY 12174
(800) 331-5267 | www.bethsfarmkitchen.com

BLAZING BRISKET

Serves 4 to 6

This brisket is made with Beth's Farm Kitchen Blazing Tomatoes Chutney. It's worth a visit to the Greenmarket just to buy it. But if you can't make the trip, then order it online from their Web site.

---

1 (6 to 7 pound) beef brisket

Salt and pepper

1 cup tomato juice

16 ounces BFK Blazing Tomato Chutney

---

1. Season the brisket with salt and pepper. Sear in a hot skillet or cast-iron pan over medium-high heat. Remove and set aside; deglaze the pan with the tomato juice.

2. Into a large Dutch oven, pour half the chutney, set the brisket and pan juices on top, and pour in the rest of the chutney. Cover and gently braise for 2 to 3 hours or until tender. Let the meat rest for 15 minutes, then slice and serve.

The Amazing Real Live Food Co.

The Amazing Real Live Food is a great case study of the new farming movement. Chaseholm Farm, a dairy enterprise, had been in the Chase family since 1935 and was running out of steam when Rory Chase, son of the current owner—who leases out the farm to local farmers—and his best friend Peter Dessler decided to start a cheese business in one of the cow barns. Rory took a few years off to study cheese making in Vermont and California, and Peter earned a degree from the Culinary Institute of America. They were helped by Ronnybrook (the very successful farm down the road), family friends, and especially their parents. They managed to buy all the necessary equipment from online sites like Craigslist and eBay or from local farmers.

And their cheese is great. The Camembert, aged two to three months, is deep and creamy, with a fresh grassy taste. The queso blanco is also excellent. The cheese spreads, made right on the farm, are superb; there's fresh roasted garlic, basil and garlic, and jalapeño. All the ingredients are grown on the farm, so the garlic tastes like garlic and the basil like it was just picked. They also make an ice cream with a high probiotic content; the probiotics aid digestion by restoring helpful bacteria to the intestinal tract.

What's most exciting is the energy these young men give to their avocation. They are dedicated to bringing farming back to life in the Hudson Valley.

The Amazing Real Live Food Co. 39 Chase Road
Pine Plains, NY 12567 | (518) 398-0368 | www.amazingreallive.com

TUNA RILLETTES

Serves 4 to 6

Rillettes, a traditional French appetizer, is similar to pâté. Try making this version with Amazing Real Live's fresh herbed farmer's cheese. It will add a bright clean flavor to the spread.

---

1 pound fresh tuna poached in water, or 1 can tuna, drained

½ cup olive oil

⅓ cup capers, chopped

1 shallot, finely chopped

6 ounces (1 pot) fresh herbed farmer cheese (fresh garlic and herbs)

Fine sea salt and freshly ground white pepper

Crackers for serving

---

1. Place the tuna in a bowl and break up with a fork until flaked into fine pieces.

2. Add the olive oil, capers, and shallots and mix with a wooden spoon.

3. Add the cheese and stir until the mixture is coarse in texture. Transfer to a serving bowl and refrigerate for 4 hours.

4. Right before serving, season with salt and pepper. Serve with crackers.

Grazin' Angus Acres

This beautiful Black Angus farm, a showcase for sustainable, organic animal husbandry, is a direct offspring of the burgeoning locavore movement in New York State. After reading and rereading Michael Pollan's *The Omnivore's Dilemma*, the owners of this 2,500-acre farm decided to eschew corn feed, and the antibiotic and hormone treatments that go with it, and raise only grass-fed cattle. As one of the owners explains, they switched from the cow business to the grass business. What's more amazing is that they learned most of the techniques from locavore sites on the Internet.

Grass is an herbivore's natural food source, so cattle raised on grass are healthier, and, by extension, the meat—free of hormones and antibiotics—is healthier for humans. But the switch to grass is not as easy as it sounds. The animals take a lot longer to mature on a grass-only diet, and keeping hundreds of acres of grass in top shape with 350 cattle chomping away at it daily is extremely hard work. Plus, all this is done without pesticides or chemical fertilizers.

Which brings us to the chickens. These birds do great things for grass; their droppings are rich in nitrogen, and they eat a lot of the pests that can destroy turf. So to refurbish the pasture, the owners use a system of roving chicken coops on wheels as well as movable fencing. They nourish the soil by moving the chickens from pasture to pasture between herds of cows. This little ecosystem works beautifully. The grass is always in good shape, the cows and chickens are well fed, and—as a bonus—the eggs are delicious. In winter, the cattle graze on hay harvested during the summer month.

The meat produced at Grazin' Angus Acres is remarkable. To make the most of their meats, the owners recommend this simple cooking method: Sear each steak on both sides over extremely high heat. Finish in the oven at 275 degrees for about 25 minutes, depending on the size of the steak. Season with salt and pepper only after you've tasted the meat.

Grazin' Angus Acres 176 Bartel Road | Ghent, NY 12075 | (518) 392-3620 | www.grazinangusacres.com

Hawthorne Valley Farm

Our road trip to Hawthorne Valley Farm was delayed by a herd of Holsteins crossing the two-lane blacktop to a new pasture. It was a pleasant ten minutes, and we were able to look across 250 acres of pastures to the thirty acres of woodland that all form part of this enormous and beautiful nonprofit farm dedicated to teaching the principles of biodynamic farming.

The center of the farm is dominated by a bright green barn, the farm store. Here you can find all the produce grown on the farm, prepared dishes, and breads. For the totally committed, you can buy raw milk as well as lacto-fermented vegetables and sauerkraut.

The farm runs programs for all ages—seminars, summer camps, and internships. All are directed at teaching people to farm according to the principles of Rudolf Steiner: no pesticides, fertilizers, or hormones; a great respect for the soil; and the creation of a naturally balanced ecosystem.

Radiating positive energy, Hawthorne Valley Farm, and others like it, represents the best hope for the future of farming in America.

Hawthorne Valley Farm 327 Route 21C | Ghent, NY 12075 | (518) 672-7500 | www.hawthornevalleyfarm.org

Gigi Hudson Valley Market

Gigi established her formidable foodie reputation by baking incredibly good pizzas in Rhinebeck, New York. In 2006 she opened her beautiful Hudson Valley Market in nearby Red Hook. Her concept was to bring the aesthetic of an Italian open-air market to a Hudson Valley barn, and from all perspectives she has succeeded.

The store's staff are knowledgeable about the produce and products they sell, ready to hold forth about them at the slightest sign of interest. This tactic is probably better than talking directly to the farmers, who, although just as knowledgeable, are notoriously tight-lipped about their work.

Gigi's is a beautiful market, a great place to shop and eat and home to a truly unique product: the Skizza. This pizza in kit form comes in a small brown cardboard box. Inside, the fixings look scant, but don't let that fool you. You'll find a thin, round, tortilla-like crust and four small plastic containers, two filled with mozzarella, one with sauce, and one with seasonings. It takes about twelve seconds to assemble the Skizza, and kids have a great time building their own. First, spread the sauce over the crust; then sprinkle on the cheese; and then pour on the seasonings. Place it all in a preheated oven. The result is a flavorful little pizza that disappears in less time than it took to make. Delicious and fun.

Gigi Hudson Valley Market 227 Pitcher Lane
Red Hook, NY 12571 | (845) 758-1999 | www.gigihudsonvalley.com

HOMEMADE FRESH RICOTTA

Makes 1 cup

This is a recipe from Laura Pensiero, the chef and owner of Gigi. The quality of the milk makes the difference, and at Gigi you will always find the finest milk from the Hudson Valley. If you like this recipe, her cookbook is a compilation of still more amazing recipes that use only fresh and local seasonal ingredients. Serve with toasted slices of bread for breakfast or with crackers as an hors d'oeuvre.

---

8 cups whole milk

1 cup fresh lemon juice

1 tablespoon unsalted butter, at room temperature

1 teaspoon salt

½ teaspoon finely chopped fresh herbs, such as parsley, thyme, basil, or sage (optional)

---

1. Heat the milk in a large saucepan over medium heat until it reaches the scalding point, 170 degrees F on a candy thermometer. Remove the saucepan from the heat and add the lemon juice. Set the milk-lemon mixture aside for about 5 minutes, until the milk begins to curdle.

2. Line a colander with a double layer of cheesecloth and pour in the milk mixture. Allow the water to drain thoroughly and the curds to remain. Gather the cheesecloth into a ball and gently squeeze out the remaining water.

3. Place the ricotta in a bowl and whisk in the butter and salt. If you like, whisk in the herbs. Serve immediately or place in a tightly sealed container and refrigerate for up to 3 days.

Milk Thistle Farm

Milk Thistle Farm, founded by the Hesse family in Columbia County, is the only milk producer in New York State certified both USDA organic and biodynamic. The cows are fed on grass grown at the farm without pesticides and fertilizers, and the animals are not given hormones or antibiotics. Biodynamic certification is even more rigorous than organic certification. It requires that 10 percent of a farmer's land be left fallow, a strict processing standard. In addition, the entire farm must pass these tests, not just the land used for a single product.

The cows here are Jerseys, and they produce milk with a very high butterfat content. In keeping with biodynamic principles, the milk is then pasteurized at 120 degrees instead of 240, which means a longer pasteurization but better flavor. All the milk is bottled on the farm in beautiful glass bottles ranging in size from one pint to a half gallon. Even the low-fat milk tastes rich.

Milk Thistle Farm
170 Schmidt Road | Ghent, NY 12075 | www.milkthistlefarm.com

UDSON PROCESSIN

Roxbury Farm

One of the biggest community-supported farms in the country, with more than one thousand shareholders, Roxbury Farm is at the forefront of the CSA movement. It was founded on 225 acres by Jean-Paul Courtens, who runs it with his wife, Jody Bolluyt.

Roxbury is completely biodynamic, which means that the farmers there aggressively maintain the health of the soil to produce better, more flavorful vegetables and healthier grass-fed livestock. When we visited, the crew was working in the harvest barn, washing vegetables in a large water bath and preparing boxes for delivery to shareholders in New York City. A huge packing list hung on the barn wall, and the workers packed accordingly: 1 bunch of broccoli rabe, 1 bunch of turnips, 1 fennel, 1 head of lettuce, 1 bag of tomatoes, 1 quart of onions, 1 pound of kale…

About fifteen people work the farm stand, and they start almost everything they grow from seeds. One of their specialties is sweet corn. Jody says that people rave about its natural sweetness. The pork, lamb, and beef are all grass fed. The only catch is that you have to be a member to try it, but that sounds like a pretty good deal.

Roxbury Farm 2501 Route 9H | Kinderhook, NY 12106
(518) 758-8558 | www.roxburyfarm.com

WINTER SQUASH AND KALE QUESADILLAS

Serves 4

You'll have to buy a CSA membership (see page 16) to get Roxbury Farm's biodynamic vegetables for this recipe, which Jody Bolluyt gave us. But if that's not possible, just use the freshest, best-quality vegetables you can find.

1 medium winter squash	1 pound kale, rinsed and chopped
¼ cup olive oil plus more	Salt and pepper
2 red bell peppers, chopped	8 flour tortillas
1 hot pepper, chopped	Grated cheddar cheese
1 medium onion, chopped	Fresh salsa, cilantro, and sour cream, for serving

1. Preheat the oven to 350 degrees F. Cut the squash in half and bake until soft, 30 to 60 minutes. In the meantime, in a medium saucepan heat the olive oil and sauté the peppers and onions until soft, 5 to 10 minutes; then add the kale. Cover and cook for 3 to 5 minutes, until the kale turns bright green and is tender. Do not overcook.

2. Scoop the baked squash into a large bowl and stir/ mash until smooth. Add the onion, red pepper, hot pepper, and kale mixture. Season with salt and pepper to taste.

3. Thinly coat one side of each tortilla with olive oil. Place 4 tortillas oil-side-down on a cookie sheet (use two sheets if necessary) and spread the squash mixture on the tortillas. Sprinkle over the top with grated cheddar cheese. Cover with the other tortilla, brushing the exposed side with olive oil. Bake for 10 to 15 minutes, or until the tortillas are crisp. Serve with fresh salsa, cilantro, and sour cream.

Samascott Orchards

This enormous U-pick farm covers two hundred rolling acres in the old Dutch town of Kinderhook. The place is so big, you'll need a map to find your way from the entrance to the picking areas. A series of dirt roads radiate from the central office, where you can pay for the privilege of picking your own fruit and vegetables. From there you'll drive along one of the clearly marked trails. It's easy to find your way to the right patch.

Depending upon the season, you can pick strawberries, blueberries, plums, eggplants, tomatoes, peppers, and of course some fifty varieties of apples. The farm is open for picking from June to October.

Samascott Orchards 5 Sunset Avenue | Kinderhook, NY 12106
(518) 758-7224 | www.samascott.com

Ronnybrook Farm Dairy

Ronnybrook Farm Dairy single-handedly brought milk in glass bottles back to New York. But it wasn't just the bottles that made Ronnybrook famous. From the beginning, they have delivered a product that lives up to the promise of the packaging: fresh great-tasting milk from grass-fed cows, with no added hormones or preservatives. A far cry from the white liquid in the square cartons that New Yorkers—in the days before *organic* and *local* were watchwords—had come to accept as milk. These days, good wholesome nonchemical milk from well-treated grazed cows is much more readily available, even in those ubiquitous square cartons, but Ronnybrook was among the pioneers.

One of the more obvious keys to their success is the animals. The Osofskys maintain a herd of some three hundred specially bred Holsteins in pristine conditions. Each cow has its own stall and mattress, and a team of veterinarians watches over them with great care. Ronnybrook keeps an electronic file of the genetic history of every cow on the farm. But after walking through the fields with Ronny Osofsky—his father named the farm after him—and listening as he ticks off the plusses and minuses of every cow, it's certain he knows each one's details by heart.

The farm is beautiful, and if you visit, be sure to get there in time for milking. Aside from offering milk in several flavors, Ronnybrook makes wonderful European-style butter. The butterfat content is anywhere from 84 to 86 percent, compared to 40 percent for standard American butter. That's what gives Ronnybrook butter its marvelous flavor. They also make a butter with cinnamon and sugar that's great on toasted brioche for breakfast. The crème fraîche is excellent, weighing in at a hefty 40 percent cream. Ronnybrook milk is nonhomogenized, so the cream floats to the top, and it's pasteurized at a low temperature to preserve the farm-fresh flavor.

All Ronnybrook products are widely available. They also have a store at Chelsea Market and a stall at the Union Square Greenmarket.

One last tip: When milk is this good, you don't need to use much in your coffee; add a spoonful at a time until you get the flavor you like.

Ronnybrook Farm Dairy 310 Prospect Hill Road | Ancramdale, NY 12503 | (518) 398-6455 | www.ronnybrook.com

Katchkie Farm

Katchkie Farm is a great example of a modern vertical food business. Owned by Great Performances, a well-respected New York City catering company, the sixty-acre farm supplies the catering operation and their cafés with fruit, vegetables, and raw ingredients for some of their proprietary products.

Great Performances offers customers what they call their 100-Mile Menu, a complete meal made of organic food produced within a hundred-mile radius of New York; most of the products are grown at Katchkie Farm.

Katchkie also participates in a CSA program, delivering their produce to the farmers' market in New York City, and offers an educational program that introduces children to the farm experience and to cooking with healthy farm-grown products.

Most of all, Katchkie is an outstanding business model for the future of sustainable, organic food production.

Katchkie Farm 34 Fischer Rd. Ext.
Kinderhook, NY 12106 | (518) 758-2166
www.greatperformances.com

ITSY BITSY TEENY WEENIE YELLOW-BLOOMING STUFFED ZUCCHINI

Christie Brinkley may have found fame as a supermodel, but she has also become equally celebrated as an illustrator, photographer, writer, and designer. But most important, she is an activist for human rights, animal rights, and the environment. Just for us, she shared her special way of preparing garden-fresh zucchini blossoms. It's less of a strict recipe and more of a loose template, to be interpreted as you like.

1. Pick fresh, organic zucchini blossoms. (Rinse well to remove bugs hiding inside the petals.) Create a lovely nest of fresh arugula on your serving plate.

2. Follow the recipe on the box of Swedish pancake mix to make the crêpes (or you can use tempura batter). Stuff the blossoms with fresh juicy mozzarella. I put in the largest piece that will fit inside the blossom without breaking the petals. Then tuck a basil leaf inside the blossom as well.

3. Dip the stuffed blossom into the batter. Then put it in your frying pan, in which you have already heated up the olive oil, and season with salt and pepper to taste. Sauté until the batter is golden, and then flip over.

4. Place your blossom on your arugula nest and arrange the tiny pancakes in a charming way. Top the blossom (now oozing delish melted mozzarella, yum!) with peeled tomatoes from a can. Add a lemon slice on the plate to squeeze a few drops over the blossom. Or if you have little finicky ones at home, you can top the blossoms with their favorite tomato sauce and exchange the arugula with pasta! *Delicioso!* One or two blossoms make a summery appetizer; 3 or 4 blossoms can be an entrée!

Old Chatham Sheepherding

Approaching Old Chatham Sheepherding along Shaker Museum Road, it's easy to believe this elegant farm is part of the Shaker Museum. Perfectly proportioned red barns built in the Shaker style cover the rolling land dotted with herds of sheep, donkeys to protect the sheep from predators, and herders hard at work, either bringing the sheep in for milking or back out to pasture. But this is no museum. Old Chatham is a living, breathing, thriving sheep dairy farm.

Ever since Tom Clark won a ribbon for his prize sheep at the Duchess County Fair, he dreamed about owning a sheep farm. But, as often happens with childhood dreams, life took him elsewhere. Then in 1993, with a successful career in finance behind him, he and his wife, Nancy, bought

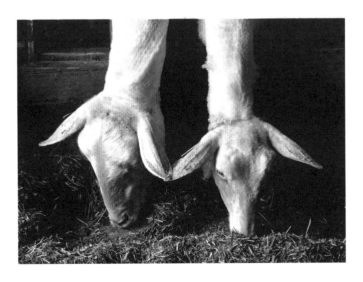

six hundred acres of pastureland in Old Chatham and have been working hard ever since, building Old Chatham Sheepherding into the largest sheep dairy in the United States. The Old Chatham label, with its silhouetted black sheep and bright green stripe, is well known in culinary circles around the country.

Everyone is welcome to visit the farm, and you can take an unguided tour by yourself. Next to the parking lot there's a minuscule farm stand where you can buy and sample cheese and yogurt.

Every barn is a new discovery. One houses the creamery. The environment is strictly controlled—no visitors allowed—but through a large window you can watch the art of making cheese and yogurt. If you'd like to see the milking, be there by seven in the morning, though if you're a late riser you can watch it at three in the afternoon, too. In another barn is the milkery, and in yet another right next to it are the newly born lambs.

The Clarks started with about three hundred East Friesian sheep and now have some two thousand on their six hundred acres, which makes for very comfortable grazing and excellent milk. Both Tom and Nancy believe strongly that sheep's milk is superior to cow's milk: It has 70 percent more protein per ounce and is also much higher in riboflavin and five of the ten essential amino acids.

In the world of cheese makers there's an awards show just about every month, and Old Chatham wins most of them for the simplest of reasons: The cheese is outstanding. The Hudson Valley Camembert reminded me of those from Normandy, with its deep, smooth, grassy flavor. The Ewe's Blue is great crumbled over a salad or mixed with crème fraîche and spread over grilled meat.

The yogurt is great, too. It has a high protein content and lower lactose content than cow's-milk yogurt, and it is also gluten free, with higher contents of calcium. For those brought up on cow's milk, the switch to sheep's milk may seem a little daunting, but in terms of taste and health benefits, it is definitely worth a try.

If you drive to Old Chatham, don't miss the Shaker Museum on the same street as well as nearby Spruce Ridge Alpaca Farm.

Old Chatham Sheepherding
155 Shaker Museum Road | Old Chatham, NY 12136
(888) 743-3760 | www.blacksheepcheese.com

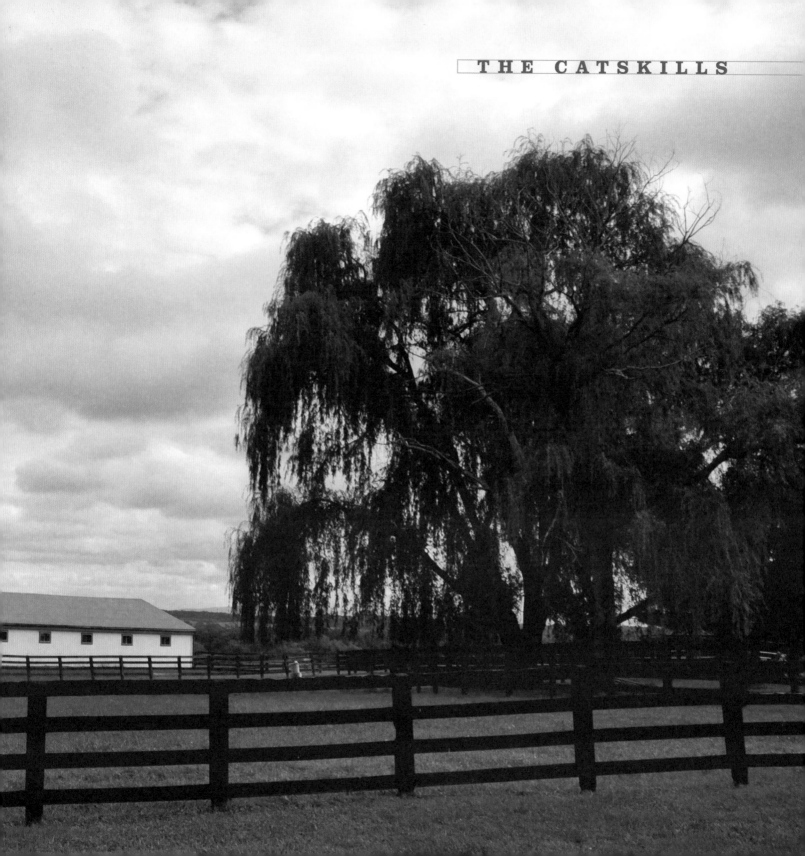

Windfall Farms

WATERMELON SALAD

Serves 4

This is one of the most delicious and fresh-tasting salads you'll ever make, thanks to the arugula and tiny tomatoes that pop in your mouth. Each bite is a surprise for the palate. The recipe comes from Chef Colin Ambrose.

¼ cup freshly squeezed lime juice

½ cup Greek extra virgin olive oil

1 small, ripe, seedless watermelon (preferably red)

½ pound Greek feta cheese

1 bunch arugula, rinsed, roots removed, and roughly chopped

4 clusters of cherry tomatoes (on the vine)

Salt

Morse Pitts, the proprietor of Windfall Farms, drives his bright green truck from Orange County to Union Square Greenmarket every Wednesday and Saturday. The truck is filled with clear plastic containers full of the microgreens Pitts grows year-round at Windfall Farms: Asian and purple radishes, pea shoots, mesclun, Mexican sour gherkins (a kind of microcucumber as decorative as it is delicious), and an amazing selection of unusual carrot varieties.

Pitts and his crew of eight deliver their microgreens fully washed and ready for eating; it's up to you to put together your favorite combination. In season, they also offer a variety of edible flowers; the squash blossoms are terrific. All the vegetables are organically grown.

Windfall is a great example of how farmers' markets keep otherwise difficult-to-sustain agribusinesses flourishing.

Windfall Farms 301 Neelytown Road | Montgomery, NY 12549 (845) 457-5988 | windfallfarm.blogspot.com

1. Make the vinaigrette by whisking together the lime juice with the olive oil. Set aside.

2. Remove the rind from the watermelon by cutting it into a large cube shape. Next cut this cube into 1-inch-thick slices. Cut each of these slices in half on the diagonal, creating triangle shapes. (Save any trimmings for a fruit salad.) Slice the feta into slightly smaller triangles, a little less than an inch thick.

3. Create individual servings by layering 2 slices of feta, followed by 2 slices of watermelon, topped with ¼ cup of arugula. Garnish with 6 to 8 cherry tomatoes, depending on the size. Finish with a generous splash of lime vinaigrette and a pinch of salt.

Mountain Sweet Berry Farm

We first met Nicole and Rick Bishop of Mountain Sweet Berry Farm at Union Square Greenmarket in New York City, where they set up shop every Monday, Wednesday, and Friday to sell their produce to some of New York's most famous chefs and knowledgeable cooks. Their farm is in Roscoe, New York, about two and a half hours from the city, and we decided to drive up and pay them a visit.

Roscoe is a tiny town, and the farm is right off the main street. No signs, just a large field, a barn, and a couple of working greenhouses. When we visited, Rick was working the farm while Nicole was down at the market. Rick told us he started farming while he was attending Cornell University, selling strawberries he'd grown in Roscoe. He is an energetic and passionate farmer, obsessed with quality and freshness. We were impressed by his dedication and the depth of his knowledge.

As we drove through the fields, we could still smell the chamomile, even though it was the end of the season. The strawberries Rick grows are small and extremely sweet, with a hint of tartness. The tristar strawberries are handpicked every three days until as late as October.

Next to the strawberries are the tomatoes, small green French lettuce, and broccoli spigarello—a very tall plant with mostly long leaves and no florets that is very

au courant with top chefs this year. When things are less busy at the beginning of the season, Rick tramps off into the woods in search of wild ramps, another top chef favorite. In all, Sweet Berry grows sixty-one varieties of vegetables and fruits.

During the slow winter months, Nicole sits at her desk and surfs the Internet searching for the best seeds, which she buys from all over the world. Rick says she is a genius at that, and everything but the wild ramps are started from seeds they bought online.

Mountain Sweet Berry Farm 159 Rockland Road | Roscoe, NY 12776 | (607) 498-4440

ROASTED POTATO SALAD WITH MUSTARD AND FENNEL SEED

Serves 6

The quality of the potatoes will determine the taste of this salad. At Mountain Sweet Berry Farm, you're sure to find a great variety and the best quality possible. This recipe comes from cookbook author Lauren Chattman.

2½ pounds small new potatoes, cut into 1-inch pieces (if large)

5 tablespoons extra virgin olive oil

Salt

⅓ cup Dijon mustard

1 teaspoon cider vinegar

1 teaspoon Worcestershire sauce

1 tablespoon finely chopped shallot

1 small garlic clove, finely chopped

½ teaspoon fennel seeds, finely ground in a spice grinder

Freshly ground black pepper

2 tablespoons finely chopped fresh parsley leaves

1. Preheat the oven to 425 degrees F. Line a baking sheet with parchment paper or nonstick aluminum foil. Toss the potatoes with 1 tablespoon of the olive oil and sprinkle with salt. Roast until softened and golden, about 35 minutes.

2. While the potatoes are roasting, whisk together the mustard, remaining 4 tablespoons olive oil, the vinegar, Worcestershire sauce, shallot, garlic, ground fennel seeds, ½ teaspoon salt, and ground black pepper to taste.

3. Transfer the potatoes to a bowl and let cool slightly. Toss with the dressing and adjust the seasonings. Stir in the parsley. Serve warm or refrigerate up to 1 day and serve chilled.

Hudson Valley Foie Gras

Many chefs believe that foie gras is one of the handful of truly unique flavors in the cook's arsenal. Yet the methods used to harvest this food have come under a great deal of criticism and scrutiny. If you have any reservations about the way animals are treated during its production, a tour of this Hudson Valley facility will put your fears to rest and allow you to enjoy this remarkable delicacy with a clear conscience, if not clear arteries.

The ducks live in a large, clean, airy barn filled with natural light; they move freely and look sleek and healthy. They roam for about three months and then are moved to the smaller feeding areas. The traditional way to produce foie gras is to force feed the ducks several times a day so that they store extra fat in their livers. Although this sounds cruel, we watched the process and the ducks seemed fine. One of the handlers explained that the structure of a duck's throat makes this process considerably less arduous than it looks. The duck's windpipe runs through the center of the tongue, so they do not have a gag reflex, and the lining of a duck's esophagus is quite tough, allowing them to swallow frogs, insects, and spiny fish without a problem. The feeders stay with the same ducks through the entire process.

That aside, the resulting foie gras is delicious, either cooked, raw, or cured. If you visit the farm, you can sample the foie gras and duck prosciutto right there, or you can save a trip and go to their Web site to order online.

Hudson Valley Foie Gras 80 Brook Road | Ferndale, NY 12734 | (845) 292-2500 | www.hudsonvalleyfoiegras.com

Beaverkill Trout Hatchery

The Beaverkill River runs forty-four miles through the Catskill Mountains, and aside from its spectacular beauty, which alone makes it worthy of a visit, it is one of the most famous trout-fishing sites in the world. The riverbed cuts through crags of black Catskill granite, forming along its course deep wide pools of crystalline water thick with trout.

The Beaverkill Trout Hatchery sits alongside the river and uses its pure clean water to feed the fishponds. The hatchery is deep, deep in the woods. (We rode for half an hour on a deserted road before finding a small sign and a few scruffy buildings; we could have easily missed the place.) The farm is dotted with small artificial ponds built to hold the fish according to size; as the fish mature, they are moved from pond to pond, always kept with others of the same size. Trout need cold, clean, oxygen-rich water, and the fish farmers here work hard to keep these ponds pristine. The biggest threat is from local predators—bear, mink, and hawks who look upon the hatchery as their personal fish pond.

Fish farming is a labor-intensive business, and the Shaver family lives and works out in the woods for months on end. The process starts in a small shed, where fish eggs and milt (soft roe) are mixed. Once fertilized, the eggs must be kept in incubators at a precise temperature until they hatch. The fry are then separated into small stainless-steel tanks. They weigh about ten grams and only a third survive, so each day the Shavers cull out the dead fry by hand. They feed the maturing fish twice a day until, after about a year, the fish reach adult size, weighing about 250 grams. Trout are carnivorous, so they're fed pellets of fishmeal and fish oil supplemented with vitamins and minerals. If you visit, be sure to arrive at feeding time; it's a splashy frenzy.

The Shavers raise several species of trout—brook, brown, golden rainbow, and rainbow—which they sell to restaurants and fish stores all over the East Coast. On the weekends, visitors can fish one of the ponds; even if you've never caught a fish in your life, you'll catch one here.

Beaverkill Trout Hatchery 22 Alder Creek Road | Livingston Manor, NY 12758 | (845) 439-4947

Fleisher's

Joshua and Jessica Applestone represent a new generation of old-fashioned butchers. At a time when more and more customers are questioning the quality of the meat they buy at supermarkets, Joshua, who grew up working in his grandfather's Brooklyn butcher shop, decided to open a store of his own, specializing in only the finest cuts of meat.

Fleisher's, on Kingston's refurbished Main Street, looks like a 1940s movie-set butcher shop: white enamel glass cases run down the middle, and big squares of black and white linoleum cover the floor. On display in the front window are chickens, all 100 percent organic and free range. They look a little strange, with their wings and legs spread wide open, but Josh believes they cook more evenly that way.

In any case, the whole store smells of delicious roasted chicken. Across the front wall a blackboard reads, "Farms We Love," and the list includes Stone Broke Farm, Davenport Farms, RSK Farm, Stone Ridge Orchards, Taliaferro Farms, Meiller Farms, Sir William Berkshire Farms, Skate Creek Farm, Free Bird Farms, Nettle Meadows Farms, Ray Toussy Apiary Farms, Stone Church Farms, Sugar Brook Maple Farm, and Twin Pines Apiary. These are the farms that supply Fleisher's. All are local, raising and feeding their livestock to the most rigorous organic standards.

Fleisher's carries homemade stocks, chicken, veal, and reduction glazes simmered for three days. These stocks and glazes are so good, you could be flavor deaf and still cook like a great chef. The handmade meatballs are certified organic, and Fleisher's makes their own hot dogs, with no added nitrates or nitrites. All the meat is certified 100 percent organic and grass fed—no hormones, antibiotics, or pesticides.

It's no surprise that many top restaurants buy from Fleisher's; the quality of the meat and their expertise in butchering are unmatched anywhere. Let them know what you're planning to cook, and they'll recommend the best cut. Trust them. I ordered a leg of lamb, but Josh told me another cut would work better. Two weeks later, I was still getting compliments on my dish.

Fleisher's 307 Wall Street | Kingston, NY 12401 | (845) 338-6666 | www.fleishers.com

Honey Hollow Farm

There's one means of local food production we would have missed completely had we not been lucky enough to meet Michael and Linda Hoffman, of Honey Hollow Farm, at their stand in Union Square Market.

Michael and Linda are foragers. They don't grow, cook, or husband anything; they simply gather wild mushrooms, ferns, fungi, and roots from the forest floor. At 3 a.m. on market days they march into the dark woods to collect whatever is edible and growing in that season. They're usually finished by about five, and then they head off to stock their stand at Union Square. They sell out almost as soon as they arrive and then return to the farm for a well-earned nap.

The Hoffmans' "farm" is in fact a 110-acre forest that was once home to a beekeeper. They know every inch of their woodlands and what grows where. Depending on the season, they can find shitake, morel, and chicken of the wood (which must be eaten very young). In spring they bring to market young ostrich ferns, better known as fiddleheads, and ramps. The fiddleheads are too bitter to eat raw, but once cooked they have a sharp clean taste. The ramps, which became very trendy after a few of New York's famous chefs fell in love with their flavor, taste somewhere between a scallion and a shallot. Subtler than both, ramps add a special flavor to roasted meat.

Be sure to arrive early to their stand at Union Square. First of all, you'll get there before everything is sold out. And second, there's a good chance you'll see several of New York's leading chefs poring over the Hoffmans' offerings while discussing among themselves the best way to soak morels.

Honey Hollow Farm Michael and Linda Hoffman | (518) 937-3998 | anteresy2k@msn.com

Index of Addresses

Long Island
SOUTH FORK

AMAGANSETT FARMERS MARKET
367 Main Street
Amagansett, NY 11930
(631) 267-3894
www.elizabar.com

AMAGANSETT VILLAGE WINE AND SPIRITS
203 Main Street
Amagansett, NY 11930
(631) 267-3939
www.amagansettwine.net

BLUE DUCK BAKERY CAFÉ
30 Hampton Road
Southampton, NY 11968
(631) 204-1701

56275 Main Road
Southold, NY 11971
(631) 629-4123
www.blueduckbakerycafe.com

BLUE POINT BREWING COMPANY
161 River Avenue
Patchogue, NY 11772
(631) 475-6944
www.bluepointbrewing.com

BREADZILLA
84 Wainscott NW Road
Wainscott, NY 11975
(631) 537-0955
www.breadzilla.com

CAVANIOLA'S GOURMET CHEESE SHOP
89B Division Street
Sag Harbor, NY 11963
(631) 725-0095

CLAMMAN SEAFOOD MARKET
235A North Sea Road
Southampton, NY 11968
(631) 283-6669
www.clamman.com

CLAWS ON WHEELS
17 Race Lane
East Hampton, NY 11937
(631) 324-9224
www.clawsonwheels.net

CROMER'S MARKET
3500 Noyac Road
Sag Harbor, NY 11963
(631) 725-9004

DEL FIORE ITALIAN PORK STORE
51 North Ocean Avenue
Patchogue NY 11772
(631) 475-6080

DREESEN'S DONUTS
33 Newton Lane
East Hampton, NY 11937
(631) 324-0465

EECO FARM
55 Long Lane
East Hampton, NY 11937
(631) 329-4694
www.eecofarm.org

ESPRESSO
184 Division Street
Sag Harbor, NY 11963
(631) 725-4433

FAIRVIEW FARM & MECOX BAY DAIRY
69 Horsemill Lane
Bridgehampton, NY 11932
(631) 537-6154
www.mecoxbaydairy.com

FOSTER FARM
729 Sagg Main Road
Sagaponack, NY 11962
(631) 537 0700

THE FUDGE COMPANY
67 Main Street
Southampton, NY 11968
(631) 283-8108

GREEN THUMB ORGANIC FARM
829 Montauk Highway
Water Mill, NY 11976
(631) 726-1900
www.greenthumborganicfarm.com

HAMPTON CHUTNEY
Amagansett Square on Main Street
Amagansett, NY 11937
(631) 267-3131
www.hamptonchutney.com

HAMPTON COFFEE COMPANY
869 Montauk Highway
Water Mill, NY 11976
(631) 726-2633
www.hamptoncoffeecompany.com

HAMPTON PRIME MEATS
235 North Sea Road
Southampton, NY 11968
(631) 287-4909
www.hamptonprimemeats.com

HAYGROUND MARKET
1616 Montauk Highway
Bridgehampton, NY 11932
(631) 537-1676

IACONO FARM
106 Long Lane
East Hampton, NY 11937
(631) 324-1107

LISA AND BILL'S FARM STAND
Main Street and Beach Lane
Wainscott, NY 11975

LOAVES AND FISHES
50 Sagg Main Street
Sagaponack, NY 11962
(631) 537-0555
www.landfcookshop.com

LUCY'S WHEY
80 North Main Street
East Hampton, NY 11937
(631) 324-4428
www.lucyswhey.com

MARY'S MARVELOUS
209 Main Street
Amagansett, NY 11930
(631) 267-8796
www.marysmarvelous.com

MILK PAIL
Summer operation:
757 Mecox Road
Water Mill, NY 11976

Winter operation:
1346 Montauk Highway
Water Mill, NY 11976
(631) 537-2565
www.milk-pail.com

MULTI AQUACULTURE SYSTEMS INC.
429 Cranberry Hole Road
Amagansett, NY 11930
(631) 267-3341

OPEN MINDED ORGANICS
720 Butter Lane
Bridgehampton, NY 11932
(631) 574-8889
www.openmindedorganics.com

PIERRE'S
2468 Main Street
(631) 537-5110
www.pierresbridgehampton.com

PIKE FARM
Sagg Main Street
Sagaponack, NY 11962
(631) 537-5854

QUAIL HILL FARM
660 Old Stone Highway
Amagansett, NY 11930
(631) 267-8492
www.peconiclandtrust.org/quail_hill_farm

ROUND SWAP FARM
184 Three Mile Harbor Road
East Hampton, NY 11937
(631) 324-4438
www.roundswampfarm.com

SANT AMBROEUS
30 Main Street
Southampton, NY 11968
(631) 283-1233
www.santambroeus.com

SCOTTO'S ITALIAN PORK STORE
25 West Montauk Highway
Hampton Bays, NY 11946
(631) 728-5677
www.scottosporkstore.com

THE SEAFOOD SHOP
356 Montauk Highway
Wainscott, NY 11975
(631) 537-0633
www.theseafoodshop.com

SEVEN PONDS ORCHARD
65 Seven Ponds Road
Water Mill, NY 11976
(631) 726-8015

STUART'S SEAFOOD MARKET
41 Oak Lane
Amagansett, NY 11930
(631) 267-6700
www.stuartsseafood.com

TATE'S BAKE SHOP
43 North Sea Road
Southampton, NY 11968
(631) 283-9830
www.tatesbakeshop.com

THE TOMATO LADY
291 Main Street
Sag Harbor, NY 11963

TUTTO ITALIANO
74 Montauk Highway
East Hampton, NY
(631) 324-9500

VILLA ITALIAN FOOD
7 Railroad Avenue
East Hampton, NY 11937
(631) 324-5110
www.villaitalianspecialties.com

Long Island
NORTH FORK

ALDO'S
105 Front Street
Greenport, NY 11944
(631) 477-1699

BAYVIEW FARM MARKET
891 Main Road
Aquebogue, NY 11931
(631) 722-3077

BON BONS CHOCOLATIER
319 Main Street
Huntington, NY 11743
(631) 549-1059
www.bonbonschocolatier.com

BRAUN SEAFOOD
30840 Main Road
Cutchogue, New York 11935
(631) 734-5550
www.braunseafood.com

BRIERMERE FARM
4414 Sound Avenue
Riverhead, NY 11901
(631) 722-3931
www.briermere.com

CATAPANO DAIRY FARM
33705 North Road
Peconic, NY 11958
(631) 765-8042
www.catapanodairyfarm.com

CRESCENT DUCK FARM
P.O. Box 500
Aquebogue, NY 11931
(631) 722-8000

THE FARM
59945 Main Road
Southold, NY 11971
(631) 765-2075
www.kkthefarm.com

GARDEN OF EVE
4558 Sound Avenue
Riverhead, NY 11901
(631) 680-1699
www.gardenofevefarm.com

HARBES FAMILY FARMS
Two locations:
247 Sound Avenue
Mattituck, NY 11952
(631) 298-0800

Main Road, Route 25
Jamesport, NY 11947
(631) 722-2022
www.harbesfamilyfarm.com

JUNDA'S PASTRY SHOP
1612 Main Road
Jamesport, NY 11947
(631) 722-4999

LAVENDER BY THE BAY
7540 Main Road
East Marion, NY 11939
(631) 477-1019 or (917) 251-4642
www.lavenderbythebay.com

MARK IT WITH G
27 N. Ferry Road
Shelter Island, NY 11964
(631) 749-5293
www.markitwithg.com

MILOSKI'S POULTRY FARM
4418 Middle Country Road
Calverton, NY 11933
(631) 727-0239

NORTH FORK POTATO CHIPS
Mattituck, NY 11952
(631) 734-2243 (warehouse)
www.northforkchips.com

NORTH QUARTER FARM
Roanoke Avenue
Riverhead, NY 11901
(516) 647-1146

SANG LEE FARMS
25180 County Road 48
Peconic, NY 11958
(631) 734-7001
www.sangleefarms.com

WELLS HOMESTEAD
460 Main Road
Riverhead, NY 11901
(631) 722-3796
www.wellshomesteadmarket.com

WICKHAM'S FRUIT FARM
28700 Main Road
Cutchogue, NY 11935
(631) 734-5454
www.wickhamsfruitfarm.com

WIDOW'S HOLE OYSTER COMPANY
307 Flint Street
Greenport, NY 11944
(631) 477-3442 (phone orders)
www.widowsholeoysters.com

Long Island
WINERIES

ACKERLY POND VINEYARDS
1375 Peconic Lane
Peconic, NY 11958
(631) 765-6861
www.ackerlypondvineyards.com

BAITING HOLLOW FARM VINEYARD
2114 Sound Avenue
Baiting Hollow, NY 11933
(631) 369-0100
www.baitinghollowfarmvineyard.com

BEDELL CELLARS
36225 Main Road
Cutchogue, NY 11935
(631) 734-7537
www.bedellcellars.com

CASTELLO DI BORGHESE VINEYARD
& WINERY
Route 48/Alvah's Lane
Cutchogue, NY 11935
(631) 734-5111
www.castellodiborghese.com

CHANNING DAUGHTERS WINERY
1927 Scuttlehole Road
Bridgehampton, NY 11932
(631) 537-7224
www.channingdaughters.com

CLOVIS POINT
1935 Main Road
Jamesport, NY 11947
(631) 722-4222
www.clovispointwines.com

COMTESSE THÉRÈSE
Union Ave/Rte 105
Aquebogue, NY 11931
(631) 871-9194
www.comtessetherese.com

COREY CREEK VINEYARDS
45470 Main Road/Rte. 25
Southold, NY 11971
(631) 765-4168
www.coreycreek.com

CROTEAUX VINEYARDS
1450 South Harbor Road
Southold, NY 11971
(631) 765-6099
www.croteaux.com

DILIBERTO WINERY
250 Manor Lane
Jamesport, NY 11947
(631) 722-3416
www.dilibertowinery.com

DUCK WALK VINEYARDS
231 Montauk Hwy (Route 27)
Water Mill, NY 11976
(631) 726-7555
www.duckwalk.com

DUCK WALK VINEYARDS NORTH
44535 Main Road
Southold, NY 11971
(631) 765-3500
www.duckwalk.com

HARBES FAMILY FARM & VINEYARD
715 Sound Avenue
Mattituck, NY 11952
(631) 298-0800
www.harbesfamilyfarm.com

JAMESPORT VINEYARDS
1216 Main Road, Route 25
Jamesport, NY 11947
(631) 722-5256
www.jamesportwines.com

JASON'S VINEYARD
1785 Main Road, Route 25
Jamesport, NY 11947
(631) 238-5801
www.jasonsvineyard.com

LAUREL LAKE VINEYARDS
3165 Main Road, Route 25
Laurel, NY 11948
(631) 298-1420
www.llwines.com

THE LENZ WINERY
P.O. Box 28, Main Road
Peconic, NY 11958
(631) 734-6010
www.lenzwine.com

LIEB FAMILY CELLARS
35 Cox Neck Road
Mattituck, NY 11952
(631) 298-1942
www.liebcellars.com

LOUGHLIN VINEYARDS
P.O. Box 385
Sayville, NY 11782
(631) 589-0027

MACARI VINEYARDS & WINERY
150 Bergen Avenue
Mattituck, NY 11952
(631) 298-0100
www.macariwines.com

MARTHA CLARA VINEYARDS
6025 Sound Avenue
Riverhead, NY 11901
(631) 298-0075
www.marthaclaravineyards.com

THE OLD FIELD VINEYARDS
59600 Main Road, Route 25
Southold, NY 11971
(631) 765-0004
www.theoldfield.com

OSPREY'S DOMINION VINEYARDS
44075 Main Road, Route 25
Peconic, NY 11958
(631) 765-6188
www.ospreysdominion.com

PALMER VINEYARDS
108 Sound Avenue, Route 48
Riverhead, NY 11901
(631) 722-WINE
www.palmervineyards.com

PAUMANOK VINEYARDS
1074 Main Road (Route 25)
P.O. Box 741, Aquebogue, NY 11931
(631) 722-880

PECONIC BAY WINERY
31320 Main Road, Route 25
Cutchogue, NY 11935
(631) 734-7361
www.peconicbaywinery.com

PELLEGRINI VINEYARDS
23005 Route 25
Cutchogue, NY 11935
(631) 734-4111
www.pellegrinivineyards.com

PINDAR VINEYARDS
Main Road, Route 25
Peconic, NY 11958
(631) 734-6200
www.pindar.net

PUGLIESE VINEYARDS
34515 Main Road, Route 25
Cutchogue, NY 11935
(631) 734-4057
www.pugliesevineyards.com

ROANOKE VINEYARDS
3543 Sound Avenue
Riverhead, NY 11910
(631) 727-4161
www.roanokevineyards.com

SHERWOOD HOUSE VINEYARDS
2600 Oregon Road
Mattituck, NY 11952
(212) 828-3426 CHECK
www.sherwoodhousevineyards.com

SHINN ESTATE VINEYARDS
2000 Oregon Road
Mattituck, NY 11952
(631) 804-0367
www.shinnestatevineyards.com

VINEYARD 48
18910 Route 48
Cutchogue, NY 11935
(631) 734-5200
www.vineyard48winery.com

WATERS CREST WINERY
22355 Route 48, Unit 6
Cutchogue, NY 11935
(631) 734-5065
www.waterscrestwinery.com

WÖLFFER ESTATE
139 Sagg Road
Sagaponack, NY 11962
(631) 537-5106
www.wolffer.com

Hudson Valley and the Catskills
HUDSON VALLEY

THE AMAZING REAL LIVE FOOD CO.
39 Chase Road
Pine Plains, NY 12567
(518) 398-0368
www.amazingreallive.com

THE ART OF THE TART
153 Knight Road
Clinton Corners, NY 12514
(845) 868-7107
Theartofthetart@gmail.com

BETH'S FARM KITCHEN
P.O. Box 113
Stuyvesant Falls, NY 12174
(800) 331-5267
www.bethsfarmkitchen.com

COACH FARM
105 Mill Hill Road
Pine Plains, NY 12567
(518) 398-5325
www.coachfarm.com

THE CURRANT COMPANY
59 Walnut Lane
Staatsburg, NY 12580
(845) 266-8299
www.currantc.com

FISHKILL FARMS
9 Fishkill Farm Road
Hopewell Junction, NY 12533
(845) 897-4377
www.fishkillfarms.com

GIGI HUDSON VALLEY MARKET
227 Pitcher Lane
Red Hook, NY 12571
(845) 758-1999
www.gigihudsonvalley.com

GRAZIN' ANGUS ACRES
176 Bartel Road
Ghent, NY 12075
(518) 392-3620
www.grazinangusacres.com

HAWTHORNE VALLEY FARM
327 Route 21C
Ghent, NY 12075
(518) 672-7500
www.hawthornevalleyfarm.org

HEINCHON'S ICE CREAM PARLOR
Route 22
Pawling, NY 12564
(845) 878-6262

KATCHKIE FARM
34 Fisher Road Ext.
Kinderhook, NY 12106
(518) 758-2166
www.greatperformances.com

THE KNEADED BREAD
181 North Main Street
Port Chester, NY 10573
(914) 937-9489
www.kneadedbread.com

MIGLIORELLI FARM
46 Freeborn Lane
Tivoli, New York 12583
(845) 757-3276

Migliorelli Farm Stand
668 River Road
Rhinebeck, NY 12572

Miglorelli Farm Store
302 Warren Street
Hudson, NY 12534
(518) 828-3277
www.migliorelli.com

MILK THISTLE FARM
170 Schmidt Road
Ghent, NY 12075
(518) 567-9490
www.milkthistlefarm.com

OLD CHATHAM SHEEPHERDING
COMPANY
155 Shaker Museum Road
Old Chatham, NY 12136
(888) 743-3760
www.blacksheepcheese.com

QUATTRO'S GAME FARM
Route 44
Pleasant Valley, NY 12569
(845) 635-2018

RONNYBROOK FARM DAIRY
310 Prospect Hill Road
Ancramdale, NY 12503
(518) 398-6455
www.ronnybrook.com

ROXBURY FARM
2501 Route 9H
Kinderhook, NY 12106
(518) 758-8558
www.roxburyfarm.com

SAMASCOTT ORCHARDS
5 Sunset Avenue
Kinderhook, NY 12106
(518) 758-7224
www.samascott.com

SPROUT CREEK FARM
34 Lauer Road
Poughkeepsie, NY 12603
(845) 485-9885
www.sproutcreekfarm.org

STONE BARNS CENTER FOR FOOD &
AGRICULTURE
630 Bedford Road
Pocantico Hills, NY 10591
(914) 366-6200
www.stonebarnscenter.org

TABLE LOCAL MARKET
11 Babbitt Road
Bedford Hills, NY 10507
(914) 241-0269
www.tablelocalmarket.com

UNCLE NEILIE'S MAPLE SYRUP
38 Mill Road
Rhinebeck, NY 12572
(845) 876-3894
neilbev81@hotmail.com

WILD HIVE FARM STORE
2411 Salt Point Turnpike
Clinton Corners, NY 12514
(845) 266-5863
www.wildhivefarm.com

Hudson Valley and the Catskills
THE CATSKILLS

BEAVERKILL TROUT HATCHERY
2 Alder Creek Road
Livingston Manor, NY 12758
(845) 439-4947

FLEISHER'S
307 Wall Street
Kingston, NY 12401
(845) 338-6666
www.fleishers.com

HONEY HOLLOW FARM
Michael and Linda Hoffmann
Schoharie County
(518) 937-3998
anteresy2k@msn.com

HUDSON VALLEY FOIE GRAS
80 Brook Road
Ferndale, NY 12734
(845) 292-2500
www.hudsonvalleyfoiegras.com

MOUNTAIN SWEET BERRY FARM
159 Rockland Road
Roscoe, NY 12776
(607) 498-4440

WINDFALL FARMS
301 Neelytown Road
Montgomery, NY 12549
windfallfarm.blogspot.com

Some Useful Links

www.justfood.org
www.nofa.org
www.rsfsocialfinance.org
www.biodynamics.com
www.nal.usda.gov
www.localharvest.org
www.cenyc.org
www.slowfoodusa.org
www.ediblecommunities.com
www.exploreli.com
www.hvnet.com

Index of Recipes

Acknowledgments

First we would like to thank each other for yet another wonderful journey together. May there be more. . . .

We would like to especially thank Ted Sann for his constant support throughout the making of this book and some amazing pictures from Stone Barns.

We gratefully acknowledge the following:
Lizzy Sann for her incredible research;
Elliott Meisel for help with the aerial photos;
Christian Diaz for his unending patience;
Shawn Peterson for his constant help and friendship;
All the farmers and shop owners who were so generous with their time and spirit;
All the chefs and our friends for their delicious recipes;
Chris Steighner, our editor, Lynne Yeamans, our designer, and Charles Miers, our publisher;
And, always, our families who love us!

—Susan Meisel and Nathalie Sann